"A part of me was writing nonfiction
short stories about things I remembered,
while another part was preserving the
lies I tell myself to ensure the truth
doesn't kill me. This book is about those
truths and the ways in which we parcel
fact in order to survive."

THROUGHOUT HER EARLY CHILDHOOD in Nigeria and adolescence in Oklahoma, Bassey Ikpi lived with an overload of emotions, cycling between extreme euphoria and deep depression—sometimes within the course of a single day. In her early twenties, Bassey became a spoken word artist and traveled with HBO's *Def Poetry Jam*, channeling her experiences into art. But beneath the façade of the confident performer, the symptoms from her childhood were building and Bassey's mental health was in a precipitous decline, culminating in hospitalization and a diagnosis of bipolar II.

In *I'm Telling the Truth, but I'm Lying*, Bassey Ikpi breaks open our understanding of mental health by giving us intimate access to her own. Exploring shame, confusion, medication, and family in the process, Bassey looks at how mental health impacts every aspect of our lives—how we appear to others, and, most important, to ourselves—and challenges our preconceptions about what it means to be "normal." Viscerally raw and honest, the result is an exploration of the stories we tell ourselves to make sense of who we are—and the ways, as honest as we try to be, each of these stories is also a lie.

I'M TELLING
THE TRUTH,
BUT I'M
LYING

I'M TELLING THE TRUTH BUT I'M LYING

ESSAYS

BASSEY IKPI

HARPER  PERENNIAL

NEW YORK ● LONDON ● TORONTO ● SYDNEY ● NEW DELHI ● AUCKLAND

HARPER ● PERENNIAL

FIRST EDITION

Designed by Jen Overstreet

Library of Congress Cataloging-in-Publication Data has been applied for.

ISBN 978-0-06-269834-6

19 20 21 22 23   LSC   10 9 8 7 6 5 4 3 2 1

For Eugie, my first love and still the most beautiful woman I've ever known. For Daddy, who has always been my hero.

For the loves of my life: Kanke, Jesam, Kebe, and Elaiwe.

All I've ever wanted was to make you
proud. I hope there's still time.

"History. Lived not written, is such a thing
not to understand always, but to marvel
over. Time is so forever that life has many
instances when you can say, 'Once upon
a time' thousands of times in one life."

—J. California Cooper, *Family*

"Perhaps it is just as well to be rash and foolish
for a while. If writers were too wise, perhaps no
books would get written at all. It might be better
to ask yourself 'Why?' afterward than before."

—Zora Neale Hurston, *Dust Tracks on a Road*

Contents

Portrait of a Face at Forty

THERE WILL BE NEW lines. New ways your face will fold and crease. Your right eyebrow will thin; the left will wither away entirely. You still have not learned the proper way to build a face. Your eyeliner, like your life, is thick and uneven. See how your cheeks droop. You will brush blush across them, etch angles into your face—attempt to contour a presumption of prominence, even as your cheekbones lean down towards your swollen lips.

Someone once told you, "You always look like you've just been kissed and left." He told you this before anyone had ever covered your mouth with theirs, but so many have kissed and left so many times since then; you wonder if you should find him and ask him to remove the curse.

Your mouth is too full of regrets to age properly. But the forehead holds spots and wrinkles and let us not forget the constellation of marks and freckles that circles the eyes. They are beauty marks now; in five years, they will be moles. There will be whispers of removal, they will say, "possibly cancerous," you will beg to keep them. You are proud of the way the night loved you so much it offered you stars for your face. That is what your grandmother told you. And do grandmothers lie? Not when she held the same face. This face she gave your mother, silently asking her to pass it on. And she did.

Only a woman so small and wise could give birth to herself so many times.

I'M TELLING
THE TRUTH,
BUT I'M
LYING

This First Essay Is to Prove to You That I Had a Childhood

NEED TO PROVE TO you that I didn't enter the world broken. I need to prove that I existed before. That I was created by people who loved me and had experiences that turned me into these fragmented sentences, but that I was, at one point, whole. That I didn't just show up as a life already destroyed.

The problem is that I don't remember much about my childhood and have only fragments of everything else. The things I do remember, I remember with a stark clarity. The things I've forgotten are like the faded print on stacks of old newspaper, yellow and so brittle that to touch them risks their turning to dust. Pages left for so long that you can't remember why they were saved. These headlines have no clues; they're just proof that there was a history, that a thing happened on a day before today. My childhood is all that ink-faded newsprint on yellowed paper, with only a few words, sometimes just a few letters, that can be made out.

My memory isn't empty. It isn't blank. It isn't dust or moth filled—it is a patchwork of feelings and sensations. The way the air smells when a plantain is fried in an outdoor kitchen. The gentle yet firm way the breeze moves when a rain is headed towards Ugep. The subtle shift in energy when a visitor approaches the compound. I don't know if it was Tuesday or May or if anyone else was there. I can assume they were, because why would I have been alone, but I also can't assume because my brain doesn't remember it that way.

I feel like most people remember in order—first, then second, and finally—linear narratives like the ones we were taught in school. I could be wrong, my relationship with "normal" is tenuous at best. All I know for certain is that my memory is moment and emotion and then moment and then moment and then what I think could have been a moment because I need an explanation as to why my heart spins and ducks when the name is mentioned or when a story feels far more familiar than empathy alone allows. I remember the minor pains and extreme joys—but I know that my brain protects me by disowning the dangerous memories. *Let's change this over,* my brain says. *Let's make sure that when we return, it will be less tsunami and more leaky drip.*

This is what we do.

⚏

I REMEMBER THE RUSTED slide at crèche, preschool, in Nigeria. The sting of iodine or alcohol when someone—I don't remember who— treated the cut on the backs of my thighs, that returns every time there is a fresh split or cut or scraping of a layer from my skin. The phantom paper cuts that go unnoticed until the blood appears and, with it, the memory and stench and sting of iodine or alcohol.

⚏

I REMEMBER MY MOTHER, her face like sun-soaked clay. Beautiful before I knew there was a word for the way her face glowed and how her smile hypnotized your own lips to lift and spread. "Your mother is so beautiful," everyone always said, and I would nod because she was something, and if *beautiful* was the word, then she was the only one it belonged to.

I remember my mother, appearing and disappearing at will. In my memory, she arrived right before my fourth birthday. I recognized her from the framed pictures that lined the walls in my little bedroom in Ugep. A photo of her standing, smiling into the unseen camera, her hair a halo around her head. Photos of her with a younger, chubbier baby me in her arms or straightening my dress or patting my hair into shape. Her eyes were kind, but sometimes held a fear I didn't understand. She liked to grab me and pull me into her, not just a hug but a signal: a reminder to us both that I was hers. Not the aunties', not the grandmother's, not the village's. Hers.

One day, during her visit, she noticed that I didn't call her Mommy. Her name is Okwo, but others called her Eugie, short for her English name, Eugenia, and I had joined them. Eugie sat me on her lap and stared intensely into my eyes. Her pretty face set with determination: "Mommy," she said. "Mommy. Mom-my." She repeated the word over and over again, asking me to join her and so I did, both of us chanting in unison, "Mommy. Mommy. Mommy." I giggled and clapped at our new game. She smiled and chanted with me. Once she was satisfied, she let me off her lap to go and play. I ran off yelling, "Mommy! Mommy! Mommy!" at the top of my lungs.

A few hours later, her childhood friend Auntie Rosemary, came by the house to visit. Auntie Rosemary cooed at how cute or small or both I was. The woman picked me up and held me to her murmuring, "Aploka. Hello, baby," over and over. "Agboyang? What is

3

your name?" I stared in her eyes with all seriousness and answered, "Mommy."

She laughed, shook her head, and asked again. "Agboyang? Yours?" Again I replied, "Mommy." Behind her Eugie sighed. The woman turned me around to face my mother, pointed, and asked, "Who is that?"

With all the confidence of three-going-on-four, I answered, "Eugie."

⋕

A FEW WEEKS LATER we stood in line. My mother's hand gripped mine as the sun laid itself across us. I remember my mother angling her body so that she provided shade to keep me cool. When we were allowed in the white stone building, she held me firmly against her. There was a sting of pain, different than the slide and the scrape of skin. This was like a mosquito that refused to leave. There may have been tears. There were always tears.

All I had to show for it after was a large scar on my left arm and a smaller spotted one in the same space on the right arm—smallpox and tuberculosis vaccinations. The TB scar shrunk as I grew, but the smallpox scar was heavy, like it was filled with grotesque secrets trying to break through my skin.

⋕

WHEN I WAS MUCH older, I learned that there were many others with their own smallpox and TB scars but someone had chosen to hide them away on a hip or back of the leg.

⋕

I REMEMBER THE FIRST time I saw the red and blotchy faces of white Englishmen and -women. They lined the streets of my village, marched down the road—looking for something or just watching us? I'm not sure. I know that I was terrified. I know that I hid and peeked at them from behind a taller someone's legs.

My older cousins told me that white people used to be brown, like us, until they did something to anger God. He turned them into fleshless, pale shells as punishment. "Look at how their skin reddens in the sun. Look at how it burns. Look at how the sweat pours down their faces and flattens their hair." They used my fear to convince me to steal coconut sweets and biscuits from the market—threatening me with "God said to listen, or do you want to become one of the white people?"

＃

I REMEMBER MY RED tricycle, a gift from my father, who was abroad. I remember it, shiny metal, melting in the sun. I don't know about physics or science or reality. It's what I remember.

＃

I REMEMBER A CONSTANT revolving door of people surrounding me in Ugep, entering and exiting without warning or fanfare. "She doesn't cry," I heard someone say. "Even when the father or mother come and go, she just stands there and looks. She's like a stone." I was not a stone. I was simply storing up my tears, I would need them later. Somehow I knew this.

＃

I REMEMBER WATCHING A yard hen struggle and flap as it was dragged by its neck to a nearby stump. I remember the ax lifted and how it crashed down, severing its head. I remember the hen headless and bleeding but still walking and moving until it finally realized that it could no longer live and fell to the ground. I remember screaming and crying out for it as I made the connection between its freshly dead body and our food being prepared. The adults all shook their heads and cooed, telling me that the chicken I saw and the one they were preparing were not the same. It was the first time the world broke my heart. It was the first time I realized it was all a lie.

That evening, I refused the chicken and the stew it swam in. "If not the meat, then eat the rest," they said. *No.* I was suspicious of it all: the soft rice, the suspiciously blood red stew. What had bled and flapped and sacrificed for it?

I pulled my lips inwards and made my mouth a fortress; it was the first of many times I would refuse my body food.

⌗

I REMEMBER A LUNCH box—thick red plastic molded into the shape of a truck. Every day they would stuff it full of beans and rice from the iron pot and mountains of soft, ripe fried plantain and send me off to school. Every day I would run into the school yard, shouting and giggling and forgetting the red plastic truck on the ground. Every day the food would spoil under the hot sun and every day I would dump it into the gutter that lined the street on my way home. A more devious child would have lied and said she'd eaten it, but I hadn't learned that level of deception—yet. So I would tell the truth. "I left it. I forgot it. It spoiled. I trashed it."

My auntie wore both fear and anger, grabbed me by my thin arm, swung me around, and delivered a series of rapid swats to my backside, before lifting me off the ground and dumping me into a seat with a plate of food in front of me.

"Gi! Eat!" she ordered.

I would stare at the mountain of food and shake my head *no*. It was too much. Maybe if she had offered me one or two bites at a time, I would have eaten them, but she was always offering me a mountain and waiting for me to climb it.

One day, instead of anger and another quick slap to my body, she began to weep softly. "Please, baby, abeg, eat. They will blame me if you don't eat." She sobbed into her wrapper. Watching auntie's pretty face twist into sadness, I felt my heart run towards my ribs and tears roll down my own face. I patted the auntie with one hand, making the same cooing noises she used to comfort me.

"Yaka, auntie. Yaka. Sorry," I said. I reached for the spoon, making sure she saw it travel to my mouth. I made a production of chewing and swallowing. "See, auntie? Gi. Gi. I'm eating. No crying." From that day on, I ate in her presence.

#

I REMEMBER A ROOM.

Maybe, I was three. Light flooded in from a window; a breeze rustled the curtain. There was an Ankara wrapper on the bed, printed with a lion on its hind legs, ready to pounce, a silent roar in silhouette. I recognized it as the same lion on the crisp naira notes stacked on the bureau. I remember my pink dress, stained and sticky. I remember reaching for the door. I remember a hand mirror and someone lying naked on her back with her legs spread. She held the mirror between her legs and from where I stood I could see the pink fleshy layer of her place. The place that I wasn't to touch on my own body or speak about. The place that, on my own body, would one day hold secrets and memories.

I remember trying the door again. I couldn't reach it, or it was locked, or both. I remember a man's voice. He was in the room, or maybe he was outside. I remember shrinking into a corner, eyes tightly closed, my heart doing its best to flee since my body could not. It was the first time I learned that when the air disappeared from a room and I felt like I was falling backwards I could find my own stillness and stand in its echo. The first time I learned to leave my body and disappear into the tunnel of my mind.

I left the flesh, trembling and sticky and small, in the room with the mirror and the breeze and the layered pink and the man's voice and the stack of money and all the memories that came before and after that day.

⧻

Not long after, Eugie returned. I remember the screaming and yelling and the sound of hands on flesh. Eugie's eyes flashing with anger, then sadness grabbing her. There was crying. And then she took me with her. I didn't know where we were going or why, but my little room and my family disappeared.

⧻

There is a memory that has folded itself into the creases of my brain and almost disappeared.

I remember shadows surrounding me while my body was a tiny, trembling ball of fever. They watched over me. I can't remember if they spoke or made any sounds, I just know that they covered me.

They said it was malaria. But years later, I learned that my blood cells were too small and died too quickly to hold the disease. It must have been something else. Something that became the blade-thin scars on my wrists and the tops of my feet—three faint lines below my right wrist, four on the top of each foot.

My parents didn't know the scars were there until I was well in my thirties. "Your grandmother must have taken you to a healer in Ugep," they told me. "We told her not to, but she must have done it while we were away. She must have wanted to protect you from something."

"What did I need to be protected from?" I asked. I was waved away.

"It's been so many years. Who can remember?"

I wonder if this is what helps me to forget. I wonder if those four faint lines hold all the memories I still can't seem to find. I wonder if my grandmother saved me after all.

When They Come for Me

A H," THE WOMAN SAID in the soft roll of Lokąą, "so you don't know your own father?"

I looked up from where I had wrapped myself around my auntie's knee and stared. This was before I lost the language. Before my tongue became a useless fish in my mouth. Before the words disappeared, before my tongue became too heavy. That was still a year or so away. Then, I still had more words than a three-year-old was allowed.

"I know him." I didn't know him, couldn't recognize him in this room full of uncles and cousins, all wrapped in different versions of the same face, but my soft mouth fell into a pout anyway and I squinted. "I know him," I repeated, this time scanning these photocopied men and boys, all laughing and shouting in that distinct Nigerian way, where even the kindest words sound like a quarrel.

None of them noticed the sleep-deprived child hidden behind her auntie's wrapper, except for one, the man who made me shrink into myself. I escaped his gaze and focused on the man next to him. A man with big arms and a broad smile. He laughed the loudest and the deepest. His words leapt from him and danced around the room. He was new. Not part of the usual mess of men who gathered in the parlor in the evenings. His face was softer. It didn't own the hard lines and deep frowns usually worn by these men now laughing and smiling. I wasn't sure if I had seen him before or not. I was three and my head held a limited lineup of faces.

The only light in the room came from four kerosene lamps placed strategically to make sure the light illuminated the room, leaving no corner dark or hidden. It was unbearably hot and the opened door only seemed to invite in more heat, rather than the anticipated breeze. Green bottles of the water I wasn't allowed to touch crowded a table in the middle of the room. I had held my nose close to one once, a week or a month or a day before. The uncle who made me shrink into myself now had been lying motionless on the chair, a colony of empty green bottles scattered around him. I had pressed my nose to it, wondering why this water caused him to shout and strike out at anybody nearby. I sniffed and immediately recoiled. It smelled like when Grandmother forgot beans for days. The water needed to be thrown away. I carried the bottle outside and began pouring it onto the red dirt.

I hadn't noticed the man stirring from his sleep and reaching for the bottle that wasn't there. I was too fascinated with how this liquid bubbled and hissed as it ran from the bottle, even if I couldn't stand the smell. It was sour and bitter, nothing like the syrupy sweet of the minerals I often drank with my food. It didn't smell good. No wonder it made the uncle mean and sleepy. Nothing in this bottle could bring happiness or kindness. I didn't see him come up behind me to see his money create a river around my small feet. I didn't know why the sky fell and landed heavily on my back, knocking me to the ground.

"See, you useless child! Is this how you waste money? Is this how you come to my house—" His words were slurred. I could barely understand him, but I knew it wasn't his house. I knew he came sometimes to see the auntie and often fell asleep, slumped in the chair, surrounded by his bottles. I scrambled to my feet, my dress covered in the sour water and the mud it had made on the ground, my small body shivering in fear, waiting for the sky to fall again. The man was a dog—an angry, hungry dog—and he was showing me all of his teeth.

"Spoilt! Useless! Where are your parents? Do you have a father?"

I felt a warm wetness trickle down my legs. I closed my eyes and left my body there. When I returned, I was on fire. My face felt like it had been stung by millions of mosquitoes all at once. My small body was inside now, the soiled dress removed. The auntie held a cold cloth to my face. She murmured words of comfort. "Yaka, baby, yaka. Sorry."

⚘

THE SAME DOG-TOOTHED MAN was now laughing pathetically at the new man's stories. "Brother, you are something!" He was no longer a foaming animal. He was a pitiful puppy. He had no bones. He looked over and met my eyes and his flashed a warning. I held his gaze because this boneless puppy didn't frighten me now. I could feel sleep returning to my body. The light from the kerosene lamps flickered and crackled, casting a shadow that distorted the laughing, shouting faces.

I closed my eyes and leaned again my auntie's leg, hoping to make myself invisible. I wasn't sure why she had roused me from sleep, but I was ready to go back. I fell into the familiar nod, welcoming the sleep tugging at me. I anticipated being lifted up and carried back to the quiet and safety of my sky dreams. I even sighed into the shoulders that held me. But there was no silence. There were hushed, violent whispers instead. The new man.

"Why is she awake?" The voice entered my chest, forcing its rattle into my rib cage. It sounded like the voice that spoke to me in my dreams. My eyes began a slow drag open. "I said I didn't want to wake her! It's too late. She should sleep. I don't like this kind of thing. Is this how you behave when we are not around?" *We.*

"Brother, I am sorry. I thought you would want to see her."

"I want her to rest. She is a child."

"Brother, I am sorry."

My eyes snapped wide open and I pushed away from the body holding me. The man with the big arms and laugh. I remembered now. "Da-ddy," I managed, and the face in front of me melted from stern into steady and soft.

"Nyono, aploka?"

I couldn't remember when I'd last seen him, only that he responded to "Daddy." A few of my uncles had tried to cajole me into calling them "Daddy" or "Papa," but I had always known the word wasn't up for barter; no coconut sweet or ice-cold bottle of Fanta would be a fair trade. Not for the way this face before me opened and exposed every tooth when I said "Daddy" now. He touched his forehead to mine and laughed again. His laughter felt like a warm breeze, it deserved that special name again:

"Daddy."

The Hands That Held Me

M Y FATHER WAS RAISED to hold and treasure family. He taught my siblings and me to take care of one another. He takes care of his entire family and their families. It can be a burden, but he accepts it as his duty.

My mother hates that my father takes care of his family. She hates how they take advantage of his kindness. They hate how she tells him to hold on to his money. To remember our family. To teach them that they cannot depend only on him. She has worked too hard for what she has and what she has is for this family. My father grew up with a sense of family.

My mother grew up always working to create one.

⧉

I ONLY RECALL EVER seeing my maternal grandfather once. I was twelve; it was my first visit back to Nigeria since my mother and I had left eight years before. I don't remember ever hearing her say a kind thing about him. She never shared any fond memories or stories. He came to ask for money. He asked my mother to build him

15

a house. This man did not raise her. He was not her family but still, she sent money for him and his children. I believe my mother built him a house.

When he died, nobody from my family attended his funeral. Not my mother. Not my father. When Papa, my mother's maternal uncle, died, my mother's grief held space in the house like a squatter. I had seen my mother hurt before, I had seen her frozen with misdirected sadness, but this was a hollowing I had never witnessed. The few times I met Papa he was stern and strict in keeping with his military training. But I know my mother loved him like a father. I know he is credited with raising my mother. I also know that whoever raised my mother must know what broke her in the ways our family couldn't fix.

My mother says that Papa welcomed her into his household like a daughter. That she was never mistreated or hurt or abused in any way. I want to believe her because I know she needs to believe it, but I've seen how they treat the children in Nigeria. I see how they separate them into "mine" and "someone else's." I see how the women of the house hold their noses at the young and beautiful, even if they are blood related. And I know how the men are. I know how they are. I know how they are. I know something broke my mother. I don't know what it was. I know there is more to the story of my mother but nobody will tell it.

My mother mistakes questions for attacks and accusations. She weaponizes her silences.

#

THE POEM BEGINS—*TODAY, I remember my grandmother as she attempts to connect with her second children. . . .*

I barely remember my maternal grandmother. I have attached every word of wisdom or demonstration of strength of character that has taken up residence inside me to this woman who holds my mother's face. But the truth is, I didn't know her. I remember very few things about her. I remember her feeding me—but that could have been anyone. I remember her walking me through the maze of produce at the market—but that could have been anyone.

My mother tells me my grandmother wouldn't take me when she left for nursing school. That she refused to even see us off when we left for America, but I like to think she whispered words of strength to me before we left. I've written about how she taught me to "carry a load." I've written a lot of things of which I'm uncertain.

Every time I mention my grandmother or what I've learned from her, I know that this "grandmother" is a character. A mythical figment of my imagination who helps me navigate my life, when I don't trust myself, I attribute any wisdom I hold to her. My mother tells me she was never there for her, "so how could she have been there for you?" When we left for America, she refused to leave her plot of land or the life she knew for even a short visit.

My grandmother was a hard woman.

I believe this because my mother is hard. Something drove her to seek another home. Papa raised and educated her. When her mother refused to visit us in America, refused to enter a plane and leave her yam farm, Papa was the one my mother sent for and brought instead. Papa was the one she bought the house for to show off all she had worked for and acquired. But there was something about Papa. Something about the way he moved, even in his old age, the way his sternness felt like more than just the remains of a military life. By the time my mother bought him the house, I was a young woman, living my own life in Brooklyn, but Papa was not happy with this: "No unmarried girl should be living away from her family," he said. Is he the reason my mother started a family before she even knew herself?

My mother told me that when Papa died, they could not tell my grandmother, his sister. They had to wait—they said they feared that the grief would kill her. She was, at this time, in a wheelchair, they told me. She was no longer able to tend to her precious farm.

What I do remember clearly is that my grandmother was strong. Physically strong. She carried buckets of water and baskets on her head with the grace of a dancer. She was tiny and skinny but I have a clear memory, one I share with my sister, of her carrying an entire tree on her head. My sister might say it was a log, but I remember a tree. I do know that my grandmother was strong—she had to be. Unmarried, three children, three different fathers in a country that dished judgment like a pot of rice. She persevered and she birthed my mother, who also learned to survive everything handed to her.

My mother is a hard woman, but she fought for every minute of life she had, so whenever she turned her hardness on me, whenever my father had to sit and try to explain to me who and what she came from, I forgave her. I forgive her always because how can you not forgive someone whose whole life was a sprint towards survival?

✛

MY PATERNAL GRANDMOTHER DIED before I was born. The story is that she died of a broken heart over the death of her only daughter. This daughter, my father's only full sister, died in childbirth. I remember my father telling me this story. It has been decades since his mother's and sister's deaths, but the pain is so fresh that Daddy's face still folds into sadness when he speaks of them. Because of this, I ask him no questions. I listen as he tells me that unlike the other men of his day, he prayed that his first two children would be girls—those prayers were answered.

As my father ages, I long to collect his memories; one unassuming morning, I offered my father a glass of orange juice and he offered me a piece of our family history in return. "You know why I can never call you Bassey? It was my sister's name. You were born so soon after I lost her, the family told me that you were her returning to me. They told me to give you her full name, Nyono MmaBassey, so I would know who she was, so you would know who she was. But I couldn't see you without seeing her. I couldn't call you without recalling her."

When my father speaks of the painful bits of his past, I hold my breath. I'm afraid that any movement will disturb the peace he's gathered, I never ask him to repeat the story or tell me the details. I never want to see my father in pain. He gave me her name—he'd prayed for her return. He got his two girls. That's all I needed to know.

I don't remember my paternal grandfather either. I think this hurts my father. My grandfather died when I was in elementary school. It was the first time I saw my father cry. My father hadn't intended to stay so long in America. His plan had been to get an education then return to his family in Ugep. But then the children came and with them the promise he made to ensure we were well raised and well educated. Losing his father was the first reminder that he had stayed too long. Me, finding every reason to stay away from home by then, was another.

My father wanted us to know his father. He told us how kind he was. That he never parented or disciplined with anger. My father told me that my great-grandfather had seen my grandfather strike his older brother while holding a machete in one hand. My great-grandfather said, "What if you had slipped and killed the boy? Then what would you have?"

My father was raised in a house filled with laughter. He grew up in a family that welcomed joy. My father told me this every time our house was frozen in the silence of my mother's anger. "I didn't grow up like this," my father would say, sometimes quietly and sometimes loudly. I don't remember if he said it when I was a child, when my mother's anger was stored in her palms, before we became too big to succumb to the pain of her hands attacking our bodies and she became too old to try. I know he says it now.

I've said that my father never beat me. Never wanted me to confuse a man's hands raised in anger with hands offered with love. But by that I don't mean he never laid a hand on me; I mean he was nothing like my mother. There were swats to the backside and thumps on the wrist, but there wasn't belts or shoes or back ends of flyswatters. There wasn't name-calling and insults that broke even the hardest-hearted of us. Still, my father didn't stop it. And he wore his own disappointment with a stillness that hurt more than any beating could. I still confuse words raised in anger with those of love.

#

I HAVE ONLY ONE clear memory of my maternal grandmother that isn't wrapped in poetry or magical thinking: I'm twelve, that first time back in Nigeria since I'd become American. My grandmother claps her wrinkled brown hands when she sees me, she jumps up on skinny legs and cries out, "MmaBassey!" and runs to me. She is small. I'm five three and I still have to fold to allow her to hold me. This woman, smaller than even my tiny mother, attempts to lift me by the waist. I laugh and resist. She cups her hands around my small breasts and announces in Lokąą, "She has grown. She even has breasts!" Everyone laughs. I laugh with them though I only know what she's said by her gestures and tone. We can't speak to one another—her English is sparse and my Lokąą, nonexistent, but she pushes food and loving gazes at me, her fingers digging into my skin. And I am grateful because I hadn't been sure she was real either.

I remember a grandmother who wanted me. I write of a grandmother who taught me how to carry a load on my head: back straight, head high, walking into the distance, and created songs to encourage me to eat, even as my mother tells me that her mother refused me. That when my mother had to go away for school, her mother refused to care for me, turning me over to various aunties and uncles and cousins instead.

I don't know why I remember all the hands that held me and fed me and taught me as being my grandmother's. I never thought of her in earnest until I wrote of her in a poem. The poem wasn't even really about her. It was about me and feeling disconnected and belonging nowhere and to no one. So maybe it was about my grandmother after all. Maybe I did know. Maybe I know that it was not her hands or her voice or her coaxing food into me. Maybe I need to remember those hands as hers because I need to remember feeling wanted as early as I possibly can.

I do know that she blessed me. I recall the way she cupped my hands in hers and blew softly into them, then pressed my palms against my chest. She kept her hands over mine and held us both to my heart. This is how my people give blessings.

◆

MY MOTHER DIDN'T ATTEND her mother's burial. When asked now, my mother will say that she didn't go because she couldn't get time off from work. But then, it was because there was no money for her to go, but this can't be true because my father attended. He went to pay his respects to the woman who gave his daughters their faces. When he returned, he left the program on the kitchen table. I saw this woman, with my face, my sister's face, my mother's face, laced with time peering back at me. She was clay-colored like my mother, her eyes the color and size of midnight like mine. Like my sister's. She was wearing a green head tie and aso ebi—you could tell that it was her "finest attire." She didn't smile and, staring straight into me, asked, "Why didn't you try to know me?" I didn't have an answer. Instead, I excused myself to the guest bathroom, sat against the wall, and cried.

My mother found me after I had been in there for ten minutes weeping, wondering why nobody had come to look for me. She wiped my face and said, "You don't have to cry. It's okay." Then she lifted me roughly to my feet and kissed me softly on the cheek.

In Ugep, you are buried in the front yard of your people's compound. My grandmother was poor. She had no compound of her own. She was buried under concrete steps leading to my auntie Bassey's house. The first time I placed my foot on the step, years later, my auntie Agnes told me, "You know this is where your grandmother is buried." I recoiled and wept. I hadn't known.

When my grandmother died, I assumed she'd died of old age. That she'd succumbed to time and the way these days pull at us until the tomorrow we didn't notice has come and gone. I assumed she'd died of old age. Nobody told me differently. They said she'd fallen and broken a hip, so she couldn't walk. They said she was immobile and needed to be cared for. I had always been told that she farmed and carried bundles on her head and I cried for her loss of independence. My mother sent money. I was told there was a roof that leaked. I was told that my auntie Agnes was with her until the end. I was told she died. I assumed she'd died of old age.

It wasn't until a recent visit to Nigeria that I learned the truth. A relative casually mentioned her dementia. That her brain had melted into just a few memories by the end. That she sometimes forgot who they were. I wondered if she remembered cupping my budding breasts, or seeing me at seventeen and trying to pick me up once more, though I was even bigger by then. Did she remember blowing blessings into my palms? I wondered if anyone had collected her memories before they'd left her.

I wonder why my mother never told me that my grandmother died of a broken brain.

Young Girls They Do Get Weary

REMEMBER IT AS 1984.

I remember it as the third grade, three months before the new tire swing on the playground. Before the contest to see who could spin the fastest and the longest, during recess, began. Before I stood in front of the class and threw up all over Mrs. Zeroski's shoes.

Google tells me that it was 1986 when it happened. Says that it was probably Mrs. Moelling in the fifth grade. But I remember it as part of 1984, the year it all began to fall apart, so I will tell it the way I remember it. With the faces and people who stain my memory. What is truth if it's not the place where reality and memory meet?

#

I REMEMBER EVERYTHING AS 1984. As eight years old. As third grade. As a year of disappointment and heaviness and worry and everything in my brain switching from steady and somewhat okay to enveloping me in a sadness I didn't understand.

#

I REMEMBER THAT EACH classroom had a television in it so we could watch historic moments as they happened and this was undeniably one. All of us, overwhelmed with excitement; giggles and chatter ricocheting off the walls. I remember our teacher tried to quiet us, tried to sneak in a lesson, tried to tie what we were about to watch into a teachable moment, but she couldn't hide her excitement either. Finally, she gave up and switched on the TV.

I remember Tom Brokaw's heavy, beautifully enunciated tenor describing the space mission we were about to witness. I may or may not have had a crush on him; I perked up whenever his voice rang from the TV at home. But today wasn't about Tom Brokaw. It was about the first teacher in space: Christa McAuliffe. The entire world was waiting in anticipation and my class was no different. We sat at our desks transfixed, and watched the astronauts walk across the plank to the space shuttle, waving and smiling. The camera zoomed in on Christa McAuliffe. She looked so normal—like any teacher at my school. When she smiled into the camera, I remember smiling back.

The crew walked to the entrance of the space shuttle and then turned and waved one last time before entering. Tom Brokaw told us that they were going inside and getting ready for liftoff. We had studied space travel and NASA in anticipation of this day, so I knew that they would strap themselves in, brace themselves. Our class joined the countdown.

"10–9–8–7–6–5–4–3–2–1

"And we have liftoff!"

As the shuttle climbed higher and higher, I could feel my body begin to surge. The room got hot and I could feel myself get light-headed.

I recognized this surge. It was the whirlwind that overcame me on nights I couldn't sleep. It was me, wild-eyed and energetic, a monster on the playground, smashing the tetherball around the pole, narrowly missing my opponent's head. It was me, in class, knowing that I had to sit still, be still—those were the rules—but feeling like something was running around inside of me so quickly that I could almost feel my blood sprinting through my veins until I couldn't take it anymore and would ask to be excused to the bathroom and would run as fast as I could there and back, twice.

It was like that, only multiplied a hundred times and more uncomfortable. This was almost painful; it felt like my blood was rushing around, looking for an exit. I had to shut out the buzzing around me. I closed my eyes, lowered my head, and did my own backwards count to ten, trying to settle my quaking body. When I looked up again, the shuttle was still steady and climbing further and further into the blue of sky. I closed my eyes again, nothing more than a blink.

What came next was something I still struggle to make sense of. I can still see the fireball explosion and the puff of smoke; lumpy like a cancerous cloud, like a misshapen, two-headed serpent. . . .

There was a quiet in our classroom, in the school, in the world, for what felt like an eternity—but it must have only been a moment because suddenly, the first child found a gasp and that gasp gave way to sobs that still echo in my ears. Everyone was crying, some with tears running down their face silently, others wailing and weeping. It wasn't until I noticed that my hands, balled in tight fists on my desk, were soaked that I realized that I was crying. I don't know if I wailed. I do know that my face was wet, and my new glasses held a river, but I think I was silent. I looked over at my teacher, her face white as the smoke and clouds, slumped dead-eyed against the edge of her desk.

I remember fearing that she would faint. I remember wondering if I could lift her. I was too stunned to think of anything else.

On air, Tom Brokaw was attempting to make sense of the thing we had just witnessed. He struggled, his voice heavy with grief and confusion. Then there was a pause and his familiar face fell for a split second before he offered the news he had just learned. "Ladies and gentlemen, *there are no survivors.*"

There are no survivors.

There are no survivors.

That lived like an echo in my head long after he said it. The teacher pulled herself together enough in time to turn off the TV so we wouldn't see the wreckage, but it was too late for me. I was already imagining the mangled mess of metal spread on the ground, the pieces of flesh and limbs littered across Florida. I wondered if those who came to watch were sprayed with debris and blood. The quaking in my body returned.

I can't imagine we just returned to math and reading groups. I can't imagine us just rolling into the blacktop for tetherball and soccer at recess. At some point, we went home. At some point, we stopped discussing it. At some point, our lives continued. My life was forever changed. Tom Brokaw's "There were no survivors" lived in my chest. I didn't understand who got to choose who survives and who dies. God, I guessed. But what were his criteria? Maybe if I hadn't blinked at that exact moment, maybe if I hadn't turned my head or if I had been better at sitting still, those people, that teacher, wouldn't be dead, those families wouldn't be in such pain. If I hadn't looked away. If I hadn't been so concerned about my own discomfort and taken my eyes off those seven people. If I hadn't upset Mommy or disappointed Daddy. If I had studied harder for the math test. If I had run faster. If I tried harder. If I was better. If I was better. If I was better there would have been survivors.

The explosion had triggered something that I wouldn't have the language to identify for more than a decade. At home, I stayed in my room thinking about famine, war, the homeless, and the sick. Listing all the ways I could have prevented the *Challenger* explosion. At school, I sat in a corner of the playground, my back against the chain-link fence watching the other kids play. I wanted to join them. I wanted to be out there with them, but I couldn't do it. My brain was too heavy.

I started getting headaches. They would begin at one part of my head then zoom to another. The pain was unbearable and my whole body would wince. But it was also so brief and sudden that I was never sure that I hadn't just imagined them. My head was sensitive to touch. They would come out of nowhere and then leave just as quickly. When the headaches became more frequent and painful, I decided to tell my parents, even though I wasn't sure if they would believe me. I didn't know how to explain the pain and how it connected to the quiet that suddenly followed me. I waited until we were in the car. I told them I wasn't the only one who had them, in the hopes that this would arouse their concern and not a dismissal or a litany of questions I couldn't answer. Instead, they asked me if I had been doing drugs with my friends. Confused and stuttering, I replied that I didn't even know where to get drugs, which only led them to believe I had been considering it.

I hoped the pain would come, so they could at least see what it looked like, how I flinched and cringed with each pop in my skull. I tried to back out of the whole thing and find a way to ignore the comet of pain ricocheting around my head.

No. It's not my whole head.

No. It's not a pounding.

It's like an explosion. Like a cancerous fireball. Like a two-headed serpent. Like an explosion. Like there will be no survivors.

"You said you and your friends have the same problem?"

"No. I mean . . . yes. I mean, no. . . ."

"Which one?" I could feel the tension build in my shoulders. I began to shake. "Has anyone been offering you drugs?"

I shrunk into myself and allowed quiet to take over. I shook my head no. I shook my head no. I pressed my head against the window and let their voices hit me, flinching ever so slightly as the pain snuck in and set off bundles of agony in my head.

I never mentioned the headaches again.

#

MONTHS LATER, IN MATH class, I finished a test early. Normally I would ask for a bathroom pass so I could sprint down hallways and corridors to get out some of my pent-up energy, but instead I turned my test over and began writing on the blank page. I wrote a list of all the disasters, personal and global, that were my fault. I filled the entire page with the guilt I carried. I wrote of the sadness that filled my days and nights. I wrote about how much it hurt just to be.

I was called to the principal's office later that week and walked in to find my parents seated inside, looking small and anxious. I immediately felt guilty for the worry I was causing, the hours they couldn't afford to take off of work. My head began to throb.

I shrunk inside myself and swallowed the truth. I told them it was a poem, something I was doing for extra credit. They didn't believe me, but I wouldn't give them anything else. The rocket of pain was already exploding in my head. I couldn't be responsible for creating new worries. I was the oldest, it was my responsibility to be easy. I couldn't tell them anything else. I was told not to write on my tests anymore. I agreed and vowed to myself to keep the chaos I carried to myself.

⌗

A STORY I TOLD: I jumped off the roof with an umbrella and landed on a kid and broke his arm. This was not true. Despite my tomboy recklessness, there were never any broken bones. Whatever I replaced with that memory must not have had anything to do with bones; maybe it had something to do with breaking or leaping. But what?

What broke?

Yaka

YOUR SISTER HAS GRADUATED from college. She is the first of the children to do so. You come home, one spring weekend, for the celebration of this achievement—the same one you were unable to complete.

You left college, suddenly, after depression and anxiety drove you from campus like a hurricane, kept you from classes and awarded you a GPA that scraped the very bottom of any list. It is a shame you wear like a light coating of dust on all your accomplishments. It makes you feel unfinished, like in your family's eyes you will never be completely whole. And in your eyes, you have never been completely whole.

The house is filled with people and food and the noise enters your body. It sounds like an aching, like an empty, like a disappointment.

Your father is your father, jovial and calming, if distracted and oblivious. Your mother is your mother, charming and beaming with pride and frantically busying herself with things so she can complain about how busy she is. You watch as she leans in to hug your sister again and again. It's weird you notice this, that you can't stop counting the times she holds her hands or touches her. But you. Your mother circles you like a bird. Not a vulture, not anything so large with such obvious intent. An owl, maybe. Or a scissor-tailed flycatcher. The state bird of Oklahoma.

You smile at the memory of you, nine years old, memorizing the state birds of all fifty states. That was when you knew she loved you. When she was proud of the books you read and the facts you knew. The way the American English floated out of your mouth. When knowing the lyrics to a John Cougar Mellencamp song was enough for her to place the label of genius around your neck. But that was a long time ago. Your smile fades with the realization that nobody would be impressed by that now, least of all her.

This is not new—you knew it before the party. Before the speeches in praise of your sister began to feel like monuments to your failures. The insecurities you brought with you are not an appropriate gift, so you silence yourself and try to keep them far from the party. Your sister has never been your competition. Six years your junior, she was your first sibling, your baby. You remember watching her, chubby-cheeked and drooling, and now she is taller than you and grown into the face you both share, hers somehow more beautiful. She holds herself with a confidence so unlike you.

You are just as proud of her as is anyone else in the room—you have always been proud of your sister—but something is different today. You are different. You look around at family and friends; you see your two brothers, handsome and suddenly so much taller than you remember, you note, how much older you are than they. They have taken to calling each other Brother and Sister in your absence. They have stories and shorthand that don't include you. The years between you have turned into chasms you don't know how to cross.

You don't have to be here. You could have called and canceled, offered excuses and apologies into the phone. You would not have been missed. Your insecurities threaten to grow wings, and this is when you fold into yourself. This is when you decide to leave.

⧣

My mother is a tiny woman. No more than five feet tall, and even after she had four children, I would still be hard pressed to say she weighed a hundred pounds. At first glance, she is an adorable, fairy-like presence, but look harder and she is fierce. She demands respect, will wring it from anyone who dares doubt her.

I've seen photos of my mother as a young woman: black-and-white shots of her laughing with her friends in minidresses and leather, high-heeled platform shoes. The woman in the photos loved to laugh, it seems. In this photo, frozen in midexpression of joy, surrounded by family and friends, she looks like someone I want to know. Maybe someone I could have been friends with in some parallel universe.

That is the mother I wanted. The woman I got, though she still flashed with beauty and kindness, seemed angry all the time. After she smiled I would do anything I could to recreate the moment, but there were times when she would pull back into herself, into almost nothing, until I could barely see her. She morphed into a voice three times the size of her body like some sort of science fiction creature. After a day of school, I would wonder who I would see at home: the sullen mother who, when upset, would barely speak to me or acknowledge my presence for days, or the one who I wished would ignore me. The one who would drive me into the closet in my room with a flashlight and a book, anything to stay out of her way. Anything to avoid the voice three times the size of her body.

My childhood became a choreography of keeping her happy. Or putting out fires. Yesterday, dishes were fine. Today, the spoon in the sink sends her into a fit of insults and threats to leave and never return.

⚓

A FRIEND OF THE family is giving a speech hidden in a prayer. He is telling the story of your parents. How they left Nigeria and came to America to offer their children a better life. It is the classic immigrant story. It is a trope. It is a stereotype. It is the truth. You've heard this story so often and out of the mouths of so many that you begin to smile to yourself as you finish a few of his sentences under your breath.

But this is also different. You look up and watch him speak, as though you don't exist. You know this is in honor of your sister and that is okay, but they speak of her as though she is the eldest. Like she is the second chance. The only hope. The one who will do it right. The one who will make them proud. Make all the sacrifices worth it. You look around the room to see if anyone else is hearing this. If anyone else notices that this speech is erasing you.

But this isn't about you. You remind yourself that this is for your sister. She has worked. She has done all the right things. This is in praise of her. This is in praise of her. "God willing," you hear an uncle say, "the boys will follow in her footsteps and we will be here again in a few years to celebrate them both." Your head snaps up again. Surely, they're hearing this. But again, yours is the only head not bent in prayer. There is a chorus of "Amens." The family friend finishes his prayer and your mother and father both speak about how this moment justifies all the sacrifices they've made. You cannot pretend to remember what else is said, only that you faded more and more into the background with each word.

This isn't about you, you remind yourself. *This is not about you. Do not take this personally. This isn't about you.*

But at the same time, it is.

⧉

MY MOTHER IS LOVED at work. Her coworkers sing glowing praises of her humor and kindness. Her former patients send her flowers and thank her for caring for them. Their babies. Their grandmothers. Their loved ones. When I'm told this, I nod and smile and accept how lucky I am to have her. I know she gave so much of herself that by the time she came home, the world had taken most of whatever tenderness she had to offer. The least we could do was not add to her headache, she would say. When I was younger, I remember her as soft and searching, a young woman who negotiated continents with a fierceness that demanded to be recognized. She was a hero who I leaned into and hoped to one day become.

I don't know when it changed, when I stopped envying the fire and became cautious of its ability to burn and devour. When every sound and movement became a quarrel. High school, maybe, is when I first notice. She went from soft and curved to pointed and fanged. There was always a fight. Her voice became her weapon. Her poison and perfume. You never knew which you were getting or why.

⧉

I'M IN HIGH SCHOOL, my mother has returned from work and I can tell by her hello that she wears the day on her shoulders. The unforgiving bosses and rude patients have worn her down. She has been a smile and politeness for them, but now that she's home, she is back in control of her life and ours.

My mother marches down to the basement convinced that my bedroom is a disaster. She knows that I'm rushed in the mornings, that I'm often too messy and forgetful to straighten up after myself. I have anticipated this march, this surprise inspection. I have cleared the mess of clothes from my floor and vacuumed and made my bed and scrubbed my sink and bathtub. Her face falls. She searches for something, anything that can hold the frustration she's muted all day. When she finds order, her body seems to soften, the weight she carries temporarily offered peace, fire calmed. I am safe. We are safe. She turns to leave the bathroom. I suppress a smug smile, reach over her shoulder and flick the light off before she is fully out of the room.

#

HOURS LATER, AFTER THE speeches and prayers, after the gifts have been given and the food dished and eaten, you have slipped away from the party, before someone corners you and asks about your plans to finish school. "You are a smart girl," they'll say. "There is no reason for you not to get your degree." You're usually good at smiling and nodding, talking about your writing and making empty promises to return someday. But today you don't have it in you. Your train to Brooklyn is in just a few hours, so if you can just stay away, soon, you can leave. Back to the life you've built for yourself, in the place you've chosen. You left college and moved to Brooklyn without a plan, only the pull of a place you could call yours, without family obligations or expectations or the fog threatening you. Brooklyn was freedom. Brooklyn is home. Brooklyn is where you have constructed your own monuments and you will be back among them soon. You just need a few hours. You return to the guest bedroom to sit and write and wait for the time to move.

Your mother comes to find you. Your heart betrays you and allows a moment of, *maybe she's come to tell me I matter, that I didn't fail.* But no. Of course not.

Her voice is sharp and already bloodied, but when you raise your head, her face is unreadable. "Where is my lamp?"

"What?"

"The lamp in my closet. The one you borrowed. Where is it?"

You search your brain for an answer. The images of the day are racing at you but you can't remember a lamp, let alone where you would have put it. "It's in the closet . . . I think."

"You think? Come here."

You remember the episode of *Oprah* about self-defense. The expert said, "Never let your assailant take you to another location. You will not survive." You hesitate before following her.

The lamp is on a shelf on the right side of the closet. You remember now that you placed it there the night before. She asks, "Is this where you found it?" It is an accusation. It is a bitterness. It is a disgust. It is not about a lamp that was moved from the left side of the closet to the right. It is just an entrance into the fight she's been waiting for.

You offer an anemic, "No."

#

I'M IN HIGH SCHOOL, my father kneeling in front of me, dabbing the cotton ball drenched in alcohol against my face. I don't even flinch.

He is speaking. "Yaka, yaka. Sorry, sorry. She didn't mean it. You know she had a hard life."

He is trying to explain the back of her hand knocking me into the bathtub, the mark the stone of her wedding band left across my face.

I nod. *I know, Daddy. I've always known.*

I don't tell him about the bruised shoulder or the aching wrist. Let him think it was just the soft scratch.

The next day, I'm supposed to appear on *Teen Summit,* the national BET show that I appear on most weekends. I am one of a dozen or more teens known as The Posse. The makeup artist asks about the scratch from my earlobe, across my left cheek to just above the corner of my lip, still puffy but not yet scabbed over. She furrows her brow and asks, *What happened?*

I avoid her eyes in the mirror and feign shock. *Oh, wow, I must have done it on accident.* I am lying, but I am telling the truth.

She watches me trace the mark with my finger.

Her grip on my shoulder tightens slightly, she finds my eyes in the mirror and softens her voice, *I'll try to cover it up.*

⌗

THE THING WITH THE lamp is not new.

She hides food. Takes forks and cups and dishes from the kitchen and places them in random corners of the house. She asks where her food is. Who finished her fruit. Who didn't return her things to the right place. She is protective of what she owns. Every shopping trip, no matter how many times a week, she returns with rolls of toilet paper, paper towels, coffee cans, soap, toothbrushes. You can find them stashed all over the house, often stacked like she's building her own marketplace.

"She wasn't treated well; worries that these things will run out," your father tells you during one of the many conversations that replaced apologies in your house. "She doesn't like her things being taken."

⧻

I've heard stories of her past. She offers rose-colored memories, but the truth is hidden somewhere in between her stories and my father's excuses. My mother's unhappiness seeps through her pores. It lifts from her skin and mingles with the Dolce & Gabbana perfume she loves—Light Blue. I wonder how much of that is a pain she can't reveal.

My mother loves and hates and heals and hurts with the same hands.

⧻

Senior year of high school, my brain has made studying difficult. For every word I read, there are five more I forget. The letters appear to move around the page when I try to hold them steady.

The house shakes with the thud of books and shoes bouncing off my bedroom walls, as I start throwing things in frustration. Mommy comes down to investigate. I imagine that she comes down the stairs with her mouth poised to shout, "Odebongki? What is it now?"— Met with the sight of her firstborn folded into the tight space between bed and dresser, her face against her knees, weeping, my mother goes silent instead, allowing any anger to evaporate. I feel her kneel in front of me and place a hand on my cheek, gently lifting my face off my knees. I wait for her discipline, for an admonishment, for anger at the noise or the marks my shoes left on the wall.

She offers a gentler inquiry, "Nyono, odebong?" Her voice soft and curling around me. "What's wrong?"

I hiccup out the story, tell her about the confusion and the fog and the frustration and the terror and the inability to concentrate and the dropping grades and the fear of college and the future and the fatigue and the fatigue and the desire to sleep forever. I'm afraid to look at her and keep my eyes on a patch of carpet just beyond my feet.

"Okay." I hear her exhale, but she doesn't say anything else, just retrieves the abused textbook from the floor and helps me up from the ground. I expect her to hand me the book and tell me to get back to it. I expect words about God and responsibility, or how she should be the one crying because of how hard she works. Instead, that evening, she becomes solid rock beside the crumble and dust that is beginning to bury me.

"Yaka," she says. "It's okay. Yaka."

My mother sits next to me and places a gentle arm around my shoulder. "What page?" she asks.

My mother never read to us when we were kids. She was too busy with work and school and trying to navigate this American space and these foreign, Americanized children. There was never enough time.

She begins to read, slowly and methodically, stumbling a few times on the words. I lean in, placing my head against her thin shoulders, and listen. The moment reminds me of the tenderness she once offered so freely, before the thing that created her own chaos overwhelmed her. Before life became about survival and not living.

###

MY MOTHER WORKS HARD. She carries her body to and from work through illnesses and fatigue. She does this for her family to provide the things she was not afforded. This isn't about lamps, or her shame over my lack of degree.

This is something else.

This is more like a war.

Her voice lowers to an audible smirk. This is about the money she gave you to pay down mania-fueled credit card debt.

She gave you the money to help you fix your credit, hoping that in exchange you would excuse the outbursts. Hoping it would offer a "worth-it." Hoping you would offer her gratitude. Offer her love. Offer a reason. Offer her ownership. Money is a tie that binds. Money makes people stay.

You were going to pay her back. Every red-and-purple-fisted cent, but that was before your world exploded, with you still in it. Before the work stopped and the checks with it. Before the shame left holes inside of you.

You hear her now.

"You don't even mention it."

You offer her the truth. "Because I was ashamed."

Her face flashes: Empathy? Disgust? "You're ashamed. You don't think I am ashamed? You think I work so hard, with no appreciation, just to throw my money away? You're just a disappointment. You don't even mention it. You just ran away. You don't even come home anymore unless you're asked." You can hear the hurt sneak in between the words. But the awareness of her hurt is small compared to your own. The words enter you and mutate into their own meanings: You never do anything right. You can't even put something back where you found it. You want to apologize for the lamp, for dropping out of school, for being crazy, for disappointing everyone. But you don't.

Instead, you turn and walk away, back to the guest room. Back to your attempts at self-protection. Back to dreaming of Brooklyn. You vow to pay her back. You will pay her back. Once you get your life back.

She follows you. Taunting and poking. But you are holding yourself. You are holding yourself. You open your laptop and take yourself someplace else. You are already on the train. Already back in Brooklyn.

Your mother begins to laugh. It is a sharp and piercing laugh. It is not a laugh of joy. She finds your silence disrespectful. She wants this fight. You want to yell and scream and stick up for yourself, but you know it will invite things you don't have a makeup artist to cover up. So you stare longer at your laptop, the screen and your face blank, until a renegade tear betrays you.

Blood in the water.

"Oh, so now you're crying? You think I don't want to cry from how you've disappointed me? Do you even know how much money I gave you?"

Of course you do. Five thousand dollars. The number circles you every day.

Then she does the thing that forces you further inside yourself: She calls your sister from the party.

"Yes?" Your sister stands at the door and looks at you then back at your mother then back at you. There is a moment of confusion, then fear transparent on her face, then the wall she's built to hold herself rises and she is no longer there with you. Your mother, the bully, wants your sister to join in taunting. "You see her crying?" Your sister refuses to laugh or look at you.

You don't blame her. This is how she protects herself. So you sit and brace yourself and wait for the blows to come or for the mouth to stop. Mommy will get nothing but the tears.

Your sister looks at you; there is a flash of helplessness in her eyes. She turns quickly and mumbles, "Mom, there are people down-stairs."

Realizing she has no ally, your mother follows her out of the room. You wonder if your sister did this on purpose. Wonder if she led her out of the room and away from you like a keeper luring a lion from its prey.

You wait for a moment. You can still hear the party downstairs. You hear your father's laughter above all others'. You wonder, briefly, if you should tell him. Decide against it. Nothing ever changes. *You know she's had a hard life,* is not enough for you this time. You slip out of the room and sneak into the basement, undetected. You sit in the corner, in the dark, waiting, for time, for the train, for Brooklyn.

#

YOU CAN HEAR PEOPLE asking for you upstairs. Wondering where you've gone. But you stay still and silent. Stare at your phone and wait for the time to move. For the train.

The basement door opens. You brace yourself when you hear her voice coming down the stairs. "Nyono . . . are you down here?"

You know that voice. The everything-is-fine voice. The nothing-happened-here voice. The let's-pretend-I-didn't-just-try-to-crush-you voice. She descends the stairs, she sees you in the corner, your luggage a fortress around you. She moves towards you and reaches for your shoulder. You flinch.

"Sorry, okay? Sorry. It's fine. Sorry. Why are your bags here? Are you leaving? Please, you don't have to go. I didn't mean it." You can hear in her voice that she is, indeed, sorry. You can hear in her voice that she doesn't know where the anger comes from. That it shocks her too. You've heard this all before.

Your voice is caught in the traffic between your brain and your mouth. You can't even look up. You find a space on the floor, stare at it until it blurs. You think of something you love. Someone who loves you in ways you understand. You focus on the spot on the floor until she gives up and leaves. You allow yourself an inhale to steady yourself when you hear her hesitate at the bottom of the steps, but then you hear the soft padding of her feet on the carpet-lined stairs.

The light and laughter above drip through the opened door and you exhale when it's dark and quiet again.

The train will come soon.

It will take you home to Brooklyn.

⌗

ANOTHER TIME, IN ANOTHER story, it is late, well past midnight. The restlessness has begun, like a low hum in my belly. It follows me through my days. I am sleepless nights. The comfort found only in quiet. I have run out of ways and places to hide. The restlessness has followed me from Brooklyn to the basement room in the corner of the house that they say belongs to me. I'm in the kitchen washing down pills with a second glass of wine, hoping this will render me still enough to encourage sleep. From the dark of the family room, I hear soft sobbing.

I use my phone to break through the darkness. My mother is on the couch, folded like a child—her small body bent, her face pressed against her knees. She is weeping. I hesitate, wondering if I should turn and leave. I understand enough of her to know she wouldn't want anyone to see her like this, vulnerable and still. I stand silently for a moment, watching her folded into herself, softly weeping with the staccato of someone willing herself to stop. We are not a family that hugs, but that evening I go to her and I gather her in my arms. She turns into my neck and leans her petite body into mine. I can feel her tears melt into my skin, her sobbing a tired rumble from her belly.

I stroke her newly shorn hair and whisper, "Yaka, Mommy, yaka. Sorry. I'm so sorry."

Becoming a Liar

1

LYING IS HOW I survive this. Parceling truth is the way I avoid a descent into stronger and more damaging darknesses. It's why I can still walk through this world vacillating between existing and not existing. It's how I turn off the part of my brain that needs to rest and let the other part take over. When I return, I lie and pretend I've been there the whole time. I say things like "I forgot" or "I couldn't find it" or "I was just kidding." Or I lie to control the narrative—deliver a well-packaged answer or joke—before a question can even be posed.

By far, the lie I tell the most is "I'm okay."

⌗

MY PARENTS DIDN'T ENCOURAGE lies in the ways most parents do. There were never any Santa or Easter Bunny betrayals, no tooth fairies or "everything is going to be okay" reassurances. My parents were often too real. Still I learned to lie for them—to avoid punishments and to secure rewards by giving the answers I knew they wanted rather than the ones that were true.

"I didn't do it."

"I did do it."

"I didn't mean to."

"I forgot."

I learned how to take the truth and bend it like light through a prism. I learned to lie beautifully. Completely. Technicolor and detailed and so clear that by the end of the sentence, I believed it to be true as well. I learned to lie to myself in the moment, changing the narrative as the words were released, manipulating details that nobody would have noticed in order to make them more beautiful in my mind. The sweater was royal blue—no, pink—no, burgundy rust and wine, as though it tasted of Anne's raspberry cordial. No, it was purple. Not the frighteningly sexual royal purple of Prince—a softer pastel like the sugar-coated marshmallow eggs at Rosewood Nursing Home's annual Easter egg hunts.

I learned to lie to save others. I did this for them. I am this lying, script-changing, rose-colored liar for them. At least that's what I want to believe—that I do this for *them*—but honestly I lie to save myself.

Lies are how I keep breathing. When anxiety over something I know I can't change presents itself, I lie in bed and reimagine it. I turn the purple bruises of memory into lipstick-stained kisses, the crushing weight of life into neck-nuzzling embraces. But sometimes, this habit turns on me, makes me contort pinpricks into amputations. A ruby red point of blood becomes a geyser—something to drown in.

I learned to lie to save and take my life.

2

т's DIFFICULT TO DISTINGUISH which lies are mine and which belong to others. Which I told to close the gaps in my brain and which were told to me to silence my questions. Which lies became the only things that could quiet my brain and allow me to sleep. Which lies sparked my brain awake and allowed me mornings worth waking for.

Which truths did I refuse to accept? Which truths did I give a more glittering edit?

#

I EDIT CONVERSATIONS AND situations as they are happening. People—usually men—tell me that I only remember what I want to, that my memory is selective. They're right. I choose to only look back on the things I can see and still remain whole and upright.

They say I make myself a victim. They're wrong. I give myself the survivor's edit. The valiant soldier who made it through the war, the person who always has the perfect retort or quip or speech punctuated with a well-timed, dramatic exit.

#

I'M NOT A PERSON who can be trusted with memories. Not mine, not yours, not anyone's. There are stories I tell that I've excavated and researched like an anthropologist, but, if hard-pressed, I wouldn't be able to access the "facts" without notes and clues. I rarely know when a memory happened. I may not know the year or who was president or who was with me, but I do know that I wore my heart in the soles of my shoes for a month or a year after. I know that when the sun casts a certain shadow on a cracked concrete sidewalk, that somewhere, in some past I can't fully access, there was a heart that broke and leaked and ran into those cracks.

3

THE THING THAT HAPPENED—I crashed the car into the garage door.

※

IT WAS THE SHOES. Beautiful handcrafted-leather Prada slides. On sale in a small boutique in Manhattan. No, Brooklyn. I was walking by when I saw them in the window. Or I was browsing in the store when I noticed them discarded in a corner, hidden among some sneakers. Or I got them online one sleepless night when the only thing that could calm me was the compulsive click of the mouse as I made my way through an online catalog.

Let's say it was a boutique in SoHo. They were simple and black with the Prada logo embossed in a small corner of the strap. I needed them for something. Or I didn't need them at all, they were just on sale. Or they weren't on sale and I didn't need them but I bought them on a spree along with hundreds of dollars of other things I didn't need, just because.

I was wearing them that day. I was home visiting my family and took the car somewhere to do something. On the ride back, I slid through the streets with ease and confidence. Turned onto the manicured, tree-lined street of my parents' neighborhood. As I approached the turn to the house, I realized that my shoe was sliding off my heel. I was almost home so I figured that I would just pull into the driveway, park the car, and fix it there. It felt like a good plan until I actually pulled into the driveway and tried to hit the brakes. The shoe was so crooked on my foot that it hit the gas instead and the car went through the garage door and hit the back wall, the one separating the family room from the garage. The steps that led to the laundry room and kitchen were the only things that kept me from driving through the wall.

My mom likes to say she had just left the garage when I pulled in or that my brother had just returned from putting something in the meat freezer next to the place the car folded. The story is funny now; the family joke.

This story is a lie.

⋕

I DON'T REMEMBER HOW I crashed into the garage door. My last clear memory is of sitting at the stoplight waiting for it to change. I know I made it into the neighborhood because there was no other way the car could have gotten there. Something inside of me was still on, still directing me home.

The last things I remember—I was at the stoplight at the intersection of Annapolis Road and Forbes Boulevard. A left turn would take me towards my parents' house. I know all of this because I was there, I remember it. I remember sitting in the lane waiting for the red light to transform into a green arrow, giving me permission to go. I saw the BP gas station on the right and the road that led to the shopping center in front of me. I remember this—sitting there, the car humming softly underneath me.

But even if I don't remember it, the arrow must have blinked. I must have negotiated the steering wheel towards the estate entrance. I must have. I must have cruised down the tree-lined street headed towards the pool house. I must have turned right onto my parents' quiet street and driven past the neighborhood pool and tennis court. I must have given myself permission to forget just for a moment—

weeks before, I'd heard a program on the radio about a woman who had confused the brake pedal for the gas and slammed into a group of construction workers who were tarring and repairing a road. The woman said she'd blacked out. That one minute she was driving and the next she was an air bag in the face with two dead bodies as part of her biography.

When I heard this story, I was terrified that this would happen to me too. I read similar stories, wondered if I could be next. I thought about the way my mind wanders, how I drift through days losing hours, forgetting to remain in my body. How they call me absent-minded, forgetful. The way I am mercury spilling over surfaces—solid and liquid, here and not. When you carry fear and disaster in your mouth, you taste it constantly like it's the only thing your tongue has ever known.

I started second-guessing myself every time I entered the car. I would sit in the driver's seat and slowly go through a mental check-list before I even put the key in the ignition. *Make sure the car is in park and lightly tap the gas and then the brake. Make sure you can still distinguish one from the other. Remember: gas on the right, brake on the left. Remember: You are the driver. You are in control. You are the driver.*

It became my ritual every time I drove—I needed to make sure there would be no bodies, that my mind would stay present enough to keep the world safe from me. *Keep your foot on the brake while driving so that the brake will be your default if it comes to that. You are in charge. You are the driver.*

But I must have given myself permission to forget, just for a moment. To be a normal person, someone who didn't have to carry the weight of ritual in her head for protection. When I returned to my body, I was about to drive into the garage, but in my head, I was *still* waiting for the red light to become a green arrow. When I returned, I was still a body waiting to go, not one needing to stop. In my head, I heard cars honk, slammed on the gas to get moving. But there was no green light and no cars honking their impatience. Just me and a foot poised between brakes and gas and I chose the wrong one. Then I was a hole in the garage door, a dent in the wall next to the freezer, a face, swollen and bruised, red with burns the air bag couldn't protect me from.

I knew immediately, even as the shock became a spiraling scream from my throat, that I couldn't tell this story.

Tehuti

"You love once, I told you. Even when
you love over and over again it is the
same once, the same one."

—Lorrie Moore, *Self-Help*

H E BRINGS YOU GIFTS.

Fabric from Ghana. Black and shiny and stiff and with no
real use. You're sure there's a metaphor here. Personalized perfume from Paris and a portrait of the Black Madonna. Bags from
an artisan in Oakland. A book of poems that returned with him
from L.A.

You want to confront him, ask him who and when and where and
why and why? But your tongue isn't in your mouth.

You have confronted him before, when he brought you the kimono
from Japan. Heavy and pink and silk. Elaborately embroidered with

either flowers or dragons. He said, "Princess, come on. Don't ask me things like that. I love you."

He calls you princess. Sometimes sweetheart or sweetie. Some days, love or baby. He only says your name when you're making love. He says it like he wants to keep it safe in his mouth.

When you call his Cambridge house from your Brooklyn apartment, you can hear giggling in the background. "That's Tanya. You remember her, don't you? We're studying."

He's telling the truth, but he's lying. "How are you? Did you eat?"

You throw the fabric away, tell him you've taken it to a tailor to have a dress sewn. Pour the perfume down the drain. You tell him you dropped it and it shattered, an epidemic of glass at your feet. He coos about the dangers of glass and tender skin. "Were you hurt?"

No.

He pulls your feet into his lap and examines the soles, looking for what? A cut? Blood? Shards of glass embedded in the skin? As though, had it been true, you would have sat bleeding and hurt waiting until he arrived to pull the slivers from your flesh.

It's okay, you tell him. I'm not bleeding.

He asks if you've eaten. Makes a production of cooking and feeding. Your mouth is crowded with seitan and secrets.

You take the kimono with you to Cambridge to visit him. You see how Tanya admires it, runs her hands across the fabric.

"This is so beautiful."

Do you want it?

He watches this exchange from the doorway. He sees her put it on and can't decide whether he is hurt by the fact that you've handed over a gift or ashamed that he has to lie about this too.

"Why did you give your kimono to Tanya?" he asks you, one night when he's in your bed in Brooklyn. He's rubbing your shoulders as if to warm them, planting soft, feather kisses across your back. You pretend you don't hear him and then pretend you've fallen asleep.

The next day, you don't mention it but you exaggerate your need for a robe. You say, I need something to throw on, hand me a T-shirt or something. He starts to ask about the kimono but the look you give him stops him. He hands you a T-shirt.

✻

HE THINKS YOU ARE magic. Calls you from the airport before every flight and after each landing. "Princess, bless this flight for me." You almost start to believe it yourself when he wonders out loud if you sent the turbulence. The airplane that had to return to refuel. The woman in the seat next to him who kept pouring prayers into her folded palms. You used to think it was because he thought you "was magic." You've since learned that guilt can sometimes grow legs and a heartbeat.

✻

YOUR ROOMMATE OF THREE months needs to go to DC. He happens to be driving there and offers her a ride. She accepts, shows appreciation for the money she saves on the bus fare. When he drops her off again a few days later, he runs in just to kiss you hello. "Princess,

I have to get back to Harlem. I need to get this stuff out of the truck. I'll call you later, okay? Eat something."

Your new roommate watches all of this. She smiles a silent goodbye at the man she knows as your boyfriend. Once he leaves, the smile drops and is replaced with a soft, halting worry. She looks at you and asks, "What do you know about the girl?"

Tanya?

"No, Zoey. What do you know about Zoey?"

You stare at her, searching your brain and sifting through Tanya, Ngozi, Nikki, Carolyn, Courtney, Mykala. There is no Zoey.

What do you mean?

"He gave her a ride back and while he was driving, she was feeding him. She's in the truck downstairs. I don't know . . . It just felt . . . I don't know . . ." She shakes her head like she wants to believe she didn't see what she saw. I know the look on her face. This is what he does. He shows you his hand and makes you feel ashamed for looking at it.

"She's just a friend from Columbia Law. She's my boy's sister" is what he tells you when you casually bring it up when he calls later to tell you he's made it to Harlem safely.

Why didn't you tell me about her?

"Come on, Princess. Do we have to do this now? I've been on the road for five hours."

You apologize but press the phone to your ear hard, listening for background voices.

⋕

HE TAKES YOU TO a party on the Upper East Side. It's his birthday or it's New Year's Eve or it's just a random Friday night in New York City. You're wearing the black strapless dress you bought at Dollhouse. He tells you that you look beautiful, his eyes inhaling the way the dress clings to your body. At dinner, you push the food around with your fork. You tell yourself it's to keep the stretch of the dress flat against your belly.

He pulls you out onto the balcony and wraps his arms around you and lifts you off the ground, pushing his face into your neck. "My baby girl . . ." He murmurs words of tenderness into your skin. You stand outside with him, the cold of the city surrounding you like a cocoon, offering you the hope of a chrysalis.

"You want another drink?"

You nod yes. Offer your face for a kiss.

He slaps your ass and smiles before reentering the noise and music of the party.

You stand, looking across the city you now call home. You are out there for 10, 15, 125 minutes before the dress that once clung to your frame begins to shrink and crush your lungs. You are suddenly dizzy, hungry.

Inside you can't find him anywhere. He's not answering his phone. You have your purse. You can leave. You can leave.

You ask a woman whose eyes shine with wine where the coats are. She points her glass towards the stairs and then self-corrects and points to the hall behind you. "Last door," she slurs.

In the hall, you're stopped by someone whose name you can't remember. Bruce? Brad? From school? Georgetown? Northwestern? Harvard? Or is this his house? Or his party? You juggle small talk, asking then forgetting questions. The door behind this Bruce or Brad opens and a woman made of polished mahogany walks towards you. Her face is tight. She bumps you or she doesn't. She is taller than you and beautiful and elegant. You are suddenly small and clumsy and wish nothing more than to be invisible. Your belly aches in agreement or hunger. Bruce or Brad sees her pass and steps aside. You use the opportunity to walk around him into the room she just left.

He's sitting on the bed that holds coats and scarves at every party. Worry flashes across his face but then that smile of his appears and fills the room. "Princess! I've been looking all over for you."

Who was that?

"That's Zoey. I told you about her. She's Bruce's sister." He didn't tell you about her. He denied her but he is so confident, you blink for a second. He sees this and continues, "You might have forgotten."

You want to yell and run at him with your feet and hands and mouth but you shrink and fold into yourself with uncertainty instead.

I need to leave. I have a headache and I'm tired.

"Okay," he says, concern dotting his face. "I'll find your coat. We can go."

You want to tell him to stay, enjoy the party. You want to slap him, wish you had a drink to throw. You want to walk out with enough of your dignity left to paste it back together later.

Instead, you let his hand on the small of your back guide you towards him and then through the party. He says goodbye to people on your way out. Everyone loves him. They complain and ask him to stay. "When baby girl is ready to leave, we gotta go." Everyone laughs. Men give him a knowing look. Women sigh in his direction and smirk. They all know. Your smile is all lips and teeth. Your eyes are not a part of this.

In the cab, you are quiet. You watch as the lights from the street rise and fall, creating shadows on his face. His eyes are closed and he leans back, his head resting against the window. "You want to get something to eat? You didn't eat much."

You want to say something, tell him you know everything, but you don't know what you know and the words refuse to arrive unless they are sure. The cab glides up the Upper East Side. You must have sighed too loudly or the truth colliding with your heart must have made a sound on impact because he opens his eyes suddenly. "You know I love you, right?"

You nod.

You have been here before. You have excused the women in DC and Ghana and Boston and now New York. Chicago when you and law school were still new. It was a new city, a new life to build, a new love to cultivate. Chicago was when he laid the foundation for the pyramids he was always talking about building. Chicago was the only time he truly belonged to you.

"Princess?"

You can't respond so you offer a blind smile, reach over and place your hand on his. You feel his thick fingers begin to curl around your hand and feign a cough to retrieve it. You watch the buildings go by as the cab slides easily through the deserted streets. He's closed his eyes again, fallen into a drunken sleep. You recognize the rhythm of his breathing—his eyes flutter and his mouth forms a perfect O. He will expect you to wake him when the car pulls up to his apartment building.

At the first stoplight, you marvel at how beautiful he is in the moonlight. This unicorn of a man. This Harvard Law with the Maxwell afro and the butterscotch complexion. The first official boyfriend. The chef who, the night you met, reopened his restaurant across from Howard after closing just to feed you and Imani. The one who introduces you as "beautiful" and "more brilliant than I can ever be."

The one who gave you permission to use your original name. "What does your family call you?" he asked the day after you met.

Bassey, you told him.

"Then I'm going to call you Bassey. Milli lays too flat. It's not you."

The one who introduced you to veganism and Ethiopian food and taught you how to use chopsticks. "Let me show you how my dad taught me." You remember the dim-lit dim sum restaurant and how his hand folded around yours, helping you grasp the chopsticks to pinch the food from plate to mouth. He was still tender then. Still gentle. Still Tehuti. He's the only man your father has ever met. You've met his entire family, including his beautiful mother and his sweet great-aunt. His brother let you sleep on his couch when you first landed in New York. You also met his father before he passed away; it was his death that brought you back to him.

Yes, you have been confident and left before. But then, the stress of exams. Help with his law school applications. Grieving his father. Mutual friends. Missing him. Later when you speak of him, you will joke:

I was with him for four years. I have no idea how long he was with me.

Ha, ha, ha. You will laugh to make sure the bitterness doesn't escape and burn your throat on its way out.

At the second stoplight, his eyes are still closed. The moon allows him more beauty than any man deserves to possess. At the third stoplight, you tap on the plastic that separates you from the cabdriver. You put a finger to your lips before handing him a fifty-dollar bill. At the fourth stoplight, you open the door and slide into the cool of night in New York City.

By the time your phone starts ringing, you are in another cab, headed to your Brooklyn apartment. You press the power button so hard it turns off without resetting. He can wait. You can't.

✻

YOU WISH THAT THE story ended there. That you never spoke to or saw him again. But that would be a lie.

He comes to your apartment all anger and flames and worry and then quiet and full of contemplative explanations. Still trying to convince you that you don't know what you know. He pleads and begs and reminds you of all you've been through. All he's been through. He shifts to blame. "I didn't know your visit was going to turn into staying. You know I don't believe in monogamy. It was too much. You should have known . . ." Then back to "I'm sorry. It only happened once. I promise. I ended it. That's what you saw. Please. We still got pyramids to build."

You remember the night in Boston when he introduced the idea of polyamory. You were twenty-two and laughed because nobody had these conversations. Entertained it for what it was—nothing. Your refusal to discuss it was your only weapon. A few nights later, he said, "I think we should see other people."

You said no.

No.

But now, his head is in your lap and his body is soft hiccuping sobs. You forgive him because he's crying and you can't take it when Black men cry. You smooth his hair and whisper comfort and curses into his curls.

⌗

A MONTH OR SO later, you're both in his new apartment on the Upper East Side. It's one or two in the morning, after a dinner or another party or a play, after you have already borrowed each other's bodies and prepared for sleep to come. He sits up. You stand. Find your clothes and wait. Ready to run. Always ready to run.

"Bassey . . ."

He doesn't call you Princess.

What?

"I love you."

Okay.

You nod in slow motion, waiting for the other shoe to be thrown at you. You don't realize that your breath is stuck in your lungs until your head begins to spin.

He's talking. Rambling. He mentions his mom and his brother and his dead father and anxiety and Professor Ogletree at Harvard and revolution and . . . Malcolm X? Winding a story around the room you can barely follow.

Now he's listing women, a litany of names that pools at your feet, soaking them.

You knew all of this already because his email password is your name—it took you three tries to guess—and once, a few months before, you read the emails he sent to his best friend out loud to yourself. You know he threw around the idea of marrying you—but not yet. "Maybe in a year. When I'm done."

When he's done.

You were brave and left then. But you were in Boston and he was in class and all you could do was walk up the street and then back. You barely looked at him for the rest of the trip. Managing the bare minimum of interactions for two days. You blamed it on a migraine or maybe something else. He was too preoccupied with exams to notice.

When he walked you to the plane terminal, back when this was still allowed, he waited until the flight attendant told him she had to close the gate. He smiled at her, disarming her, charm floating from his smile to her eyes and back again.

"This is my princess." He turned his smile on you. "She's leaving me. I want to make sure I say goodbye."

You heard the flight attendant sigh. You knew she thought you were lucky to have him. For a moment, you forgot that you were brave and tried to feel lucky. You remembered he loved you. This is how he is. This is what he does.

But when your plane landed, you remembered and shut him out. You knew this would hurt him. You've learned that anything that makes him feel abandoned rips at him. You ignored his emails and calls. Let him believe you'd slept with the coworker. Listened to his pleading voicemails and refused to respond to his accusatory questions. You can be just as cruel. He called every friend of yours he knew to find out why. Sent emails begging you to return to him. Then Anya told him about the emails you'd read and he went from grief-stricken victim to clemency-granting martyr.

"You violated my privacy, but I forgive you."

#

So when he stands in front of you, in this bedroom on the Upper East Side, you know all of this already, but you've never heard it all at once. Not from him. Not in detail. Not about the showers and backseats and Navy Pier and his brother's couch and the student from Accra and the Bronx.

All you can say is, Who the fuck goes to the Bronx?

He's telling you about the time he disappeared in DC and that time in Chicago before you'd had cell phones when the landline was disconnected and you didn't hear from him for almost two weeks and he wasn't studying and that's not Bruce's or Brad's sister.

And then he mentions one that makes you pause. When he was in Chicago at Northwestern. "My classmate is coming down from Chicago for an interview. She needs a place to stay . . ."

The voice in your head mocks you—*Chicago is the only time he truly belonged to you.*

You begin to laugh. And your laughter makes him freeze. Your shoulders are shaking, tears streaming down your face. You laugh until you are gasping for breath. Until you are choking. He begins to laugh along nervously, places his arms around your waist and pulls you closer to him. He holds you like you're a toddler squirming to be free. You laugh until your body explodes into tears: painful, heaving sobs. You laugh and cry and then laugh about how crying and laughing feel the same to a fragile body. Then he is wrapping himself around you, the weight of his body—of his love—twisting your spine. Everything is wet and tense. He pulls you onto the bed, holding you until you stop struggling. And then there is a frantic and desperate clawing and crying and tugging and pulling and pushing what's left of you into something that makes sense.

When you're done, he rolls over and stares at the ceiling, pulling you into the curve of his body. The sun starts to make its way over the buildings and across Manhattan.

You begin to get out of the bed and his arm tightens around you. "Where are you going?"

To the bathroom.

He sits up, tries to pull you towards him.

Michael, I gotta pee.

You only call him Michael around his colleagues and school friends. Your first time visiting him in Chicago, you noted how different "law school" had made him. You joked about how easy Tehuti was to fall in love with and how it would take more time to fall for Michael. So it's the shock of the easy "Michael" that relaxes his grip on your shoulder. You escape his arm without looking at him and search for your clothes. You go to the bathroom to wash your face. In the mirror, your eyes are red and swollen like the sun rising outside the window. When you exit the bathroom, he's leaning against the wall waiting for you.

His eyes tug at you, begging for you to reach out to him, wanting you to soften and gather him into your arms and kiss him and forget that you know. Hoping to still be only suspicions and oddly timed gifts. But you can't forget, there is no more room for you to pretend. You hate him for this truth he's attacked you with so, for the first time, you fight back. You leap at him with your feet and your fists, and rip at him and scream. He picks you up easily despite how hard you struggle and carries you into the bedroom.

When he tells the story, he likes to say that you threatened him with a pair of scissors.

You didn't. Just clothes and pillows and your fists and feet and mouth. When there is nothing left to throw, you accept the quiet.

He won't let you leave. Stands between you and the door. You are calm now.

Let me go, you say. Your voice is a hollow and a hurting.

He stays at the door.

Let me go. This time louder.

He doesn't budge.

You step up to his six feet with every inch of your five feet, three inches and 110 pounds, your hands in balls at your sides. You stare at him, your fury matching his silence. He steps aside at last and you grab your bag from the floor. He knows better than to follow you, but he does anyway, watching. Down the stairs, into the lobby, onto the street. You flag a taxi and he tells it to keep moving. You flag another and another and another.

Please. Let me go, Michael.

You watch the fight leave his body as he stops the next cab. He holds the door open, leans into the window, and tells the driver, "Take care of her, okay? You're carrying precious cargo."

The driver grunts.

"Please call me when—" You close the door before he finishes and tell the driver to go.

Back in Brooklyn you exit the car in a daze and don't notice that you've left your bag in the cab until it's halfway down the street. You don't want it anyway. Nothing in there belongs to you anymore. Not the wallet. Not the phone. Not even that black strapless dress that clings to your body. None of it is yours.

✳

YOU STAY IN BED for the rest of the week; call out sick from work. You deny yourself comfort. Punish yourself by refusing your body food. Become a person who doesn't sleep. Instead you lie in bed waiting for the life to drain out of you like the imperceptible leak of a tire.

When you return to work, you are all hollowed bones and sharp angles. You duck into the restroom from time to time to break apart. Your friend and co-worker, Maysan, walks you out of the building when she finds you frozen against a stall.

She hates him as much as you should.

That weekend, he comes to the apartment on his way to a wedding in Brooklyn. Someone must have called him and told him that you were doing your best to disappear. He wants you to eat. You want to become nothing. He sits against the wall and watches you cry. He's quiet except for the soft thud of his head against the wall.

That is the final goodbye.

⑅

THAT WINTER OR SPRING or summer or fall you experience an emptying so severe that your body becomes brittle, a husk waiting for a strong wind or a heavy rain to carry you away. You are there, a person who works and walks and exists, but you aren't. When you pass a familiar street or hear that song, your chest tightens and your lungs freeze, while the rest of your body feels like someone has lit a fire above you, like you're standing too close to an uncovered furnace.

Everything you know about this new city is because of him. You are in New York City, more or less, because of him. How are you supposed to survive this here, alone?

✶

HE LEAVES YOU A voicemail: "I saw you outside of the Zen Palate. You didn't have to run off like that. I don't understand why we can't be friends. . . . We're going to see each other around. . . . You left *me*, remember?"

✶

YOU SEE HIM A year later, after you've convinced yourself you no longer care. You're onstage at the restaurant owned by Ashford & Simpson. You didn't want to take the gig because you know he's friends with the manager or the owner's son. Somebody. But you risk it. You need the money. This is before the TV or the tour. He enters with a woman. You recognize her, a model. You hope he doesn't see you, but you're onstage so you're kind of there to be seen. Your words freeze in your throat, and you stumble to the end of the poem. You banter and laugh to cover it up.

He heckles you. Requests his favorite poem like you're a jukebox and not a person he helped break.

Your mouth opens to say something sassy and smart back to him, but when you look up, she snuggles closer to him and places her head on his shoulder. He grabs her hand and holds it. You imagine he calls her princess.

No.

Queen.

You open your mouth like a dying fish and pray words come out. Your brain betrays you and begins the poem he threw at you. The audience stands and claps, and you run offstage and through the back without stopping. Without your money. Without anything. In the cab, you wait for your phone to ring with his name, but he was two phones and a new number ago.

He can't reach you, and right now, you can't remember if this is what you need.

The Quiet Before

WE WERE TWO PEOPLE who knew enough about hurt people who hurt people to pour our hurt into a pot we could watch over together. Together we prevented the melting. The boiling over. We agreed to take on the labor of helping each other heal. It was business. There may have been a contract. There was no contract, just trust built early and adhered to like ritual.

You could say we avoided our pain. We said we were avoiding the cliché of rebounds and found warmth in each other. Derek was my mourning.

✳

"BASS?"

I remember how badly I wanted to respond. How badly I wanted to tell him I was scared. That I didn't understand why something so small had punctured me. I wanted to give a reason that could help him help me understand why this was happening. But the words twisted and fled.

"Bass?"

The phone gripped so tightly I could feel dents forming, red against my palms. The wood of the cabinet pressed hard against my spine. The marble tile of the kitchen floor digging into my tailbone. I took turns alternately pinching and twisting the thin skin on the underside of my wrist. I needed to keep myself in the room. Present. The pain and pinch reminded me that I was real, that everything had to remain real.

"Bass?"

Derek's voice rumbled through the phone, deep, not like rolling thunder or the underside of a kick drum, but bottomless, like an open possibility, like it would hold you forever, like endless comfort. The landline receiver pressed against my head until my ear reddened with pain. I needed everything to remain real.

"Bass?"

Every time he said it pulled me back into the present, back to my hiccuping and gasping. The time in between could have been an hour or less than five minutes. I just know it as an echo. Sound bouncing against the window and wall before laying itself at my feet.

"Bass. . . . Bass. . . .

"Bassey!"

Derek's voice was a road map out of a dark and dizzying forest; I only had to follow it.

✳

IN THE NIGHTS WHEN sleep refused me, it was Derek who recognized what my restlessness needed. He learned to lean in and away, holding me steady and upright, fooling me into safety and balance. He made me believe I was standing on my own.

There were moments when I became fire and flame, both warning and warming, and he would smile when I reached for him, pulling him into me. His presence was a sedative for my restless body—his bed a padded wall, his embrace a straitjacket—but he was also always quietly concerned. Never sure where to draw the line: when the energy needed to be contained or when I offered my body too readily, too quickly. Sex as an answer before any questions could even be raised held concern as well.

Derek came before Jason and soon after Michael. This unholy trinity—the father, the son, and the holy ghosted. They are the only three worth the words and time spent creating them.

Derek is the only one who is still worthy of fondness and the only one who was never officially anything more than a friend.

彬

"ARE YOU THERE?"

No.

"Bass? Are you there?"

No. I think I'm dead.

My heart had no rhythm. It rushed and slowed with no respect or regard for the rules of proper metronome.

"What?"

I forgot. I forgot. I forgot. I forgot. I forgot. My voice echoed or I couldn't stop repeating myself. It all sounded empty. I forgot. forgot. forgot. forgot.

"What did you forget, Bass?"

⋕

DEREK ONCE TOLD ME about the first time he saw me—at a party at the commuter caf in college. We were in my bed, in Brooklyn. We had spent the evening flirting between honoring our friendship and taking it a step further, and he said, "You were winding, dancing to a Buju Banton tune then you hit this split and bounce that made all the dudes in the room jump back like, *'Daaaamnn!'*

"That's when I knew," he said. "Yo! I need to meet *her.*"

I don't remember if we actually met that night, but I do remember that party, that split and bounce. I remember the way the boys looked at me and how it scared and thrilled me all at once. I'd lived a life unseen by "boys." I'd never been the right type of pretty or the appropriate amount of confident. I'd thought I wanted the attention, but in that moment it felt damp and heavy, like a towel pulled too early from a dryer. I foolishly thought it was because I was a good dancer.

It was just dancing for me. Just a way to move and release some of the energy that kept me awake most nights. But it wasn't sexual, I told Derek when he reminded me of it. It was just dancing.

"Okay." He laughed into the dip of my neck.

No, seriously.

"Okay." He laughed into my mouth before planting soft, deliberate kisses on my lips.

College had been full of those moments when I did something or other without realizing that it had its own signal, its own message. That it invited strangers to protect me, to treat me like a younger sister, even if I was the same age or older, or invited a very different type of call. I never learned when to answer and when to walk away.

Derek was different. Derek saw me. He may not have understood what he saw—but he saw me. Derek was kind to me in ways I couldn't make sense of. I'm sure he had his reasons, perhaps the memory of the split and booty bounce at the party in the commuter caf, but that doesn't seem like enough. He used to laugh over the sound of me jumping to lower the shower nozzle but he never made me feel too small for him. Other men discarded me when my moods became hurricane or drought with no in-between. I was too difficult. I was too big. I was too small. I was "too much." But Derek was always there.

Derek was there on the other end of the phone, over the bridge, across the city into Manhattan. The 2 train to Spanish Harlem. Me in Flatbush. Flat against the floor. Wailing and waiting for something.

✳

"Do you need me to come?"

I forgot the kettle.

"What?"

There's a choreography to controlling panic. A way to steady the voice and regulate the urgency. *Stay calm.* I rubbed my wrists together. It soothed and steadied. *Stay calm. Try again.*

I forgot the kettle.

"What kettle, Bass?"

His voice was calm. It provided safety for me in that moment. He knew this. I had never called or come to him this way before. There had never been tears. Never a sobbing. Never this long for the words to form and become what they needed. Usually, Derek's job was to catch the words I threw at him, sometimes, from the shower, "Write this down before I forget it. No. I'll do it."

He kept a pen and pad on his nightstand for these moments. He would watch as I dripped across his studio floor and the few words I didn't want to forget turned into whole poems within minutes. He would watch as I darted around his apartment talking, always talking. Saying something. Saying something. Saying everything. I had to say it before I forgot. I was only still when I slept and unless it was to reach for him. To feel his weight. I needed it to steady me. I needed him to steady me.

✳

THERE IS A CHOREOGRAPHY to panic. A way to steady the voice and regulate the urgency. *Calm. Stay calm.* But I could feel the panic settle into me: Mine. His. I could hear it in his voice but could do nothing to calm it. I was no longer there.

I needed to tell him about the noodles I'd lost in the hall closet. Or how the house phone had ended up in the freezer. Or how I sometimes struggled to make memories. How many times I walked from Brooklyn to Manhattan hoping to tire out my body or the voices so sleep would find its way to me. The nights I ended up at his apartment—searching for a lighthouse in a storm I couldn't contain. Derek was port. I couldn't keep crashing into him.

Derek was getting his PhD in history. He was professorial, fastidious, and tidy; precise and orderly. I tried to clean up after myself but I was careless and absentminded—concerned more with hiding the mess than with preventing it. He called me one day, upon his return from a trip home, his voice low with irritation. "Hair and Cheeto dust, Bass . . ."

It wasn't my hair, I countered.

"You inviting other niggas to my crib?"

I dismissed his question with a laugh. That didn't help. Derek would do that, get irritated with me, but it would be a low frequency, a humming in the back of his throat. He never shouted or raised his voice or made me afraid to return to him.

Derek was the only one you never had to convince. Not to say that he loved you or that love ever entered a room you both occupied, but there was a kindness, a care that refused your attempts to find something beautiful and break it. Derek was beauty.

With Derek there was never a fear of being too much or too little. No conversation that challenged the way you breathed. No discrepancy or faded memory. No attempt to convince you that what was wasn't or what did hadn't happened.

Derek was a necessary and sentient truth. He was a tenderness, an unearned kindness. There was never worry of him turning to ash in your hands. So you did what you had to and you left him before you broke and buried him.

He is the only one I regret being too broken for. If I could have allowed myself to love him, maybe this life would have shaped itself differently. Maybe I wouldn't have had to wait to break. Maybe I wouldn't have broken at all. Or fallen. Or maybe he would have caught me. Or maybe I would have destroyed him.

I think I would have destroyed him.

#

ON THE PHONE. ON the kitchen floor, in a steady decline.

His panic was patient, quiet, calm.

I forgot I was making tea, I finally told him. The kettle melted. The whole thing.

It had melted into a grotesque unrecognizable. It became tar. A molten mess, stiff and hard and plastered to the stove.

I hadn't realized, not until I smelled the stench of burning plastic and then noticed the kitchen engulfed in smoke. I saw the lonely coffee mug and the tea bag, dry and waiting. I must have been making tea. I must have put water on to boil. But all I remembered was the cold crawling in from the kitchen window. The need for a sweater or sweatshirt. The searching through the closet. The discovery of a dress I'd forgotten I owned but now needed to try on. The shoes that would work. The shoes that didn't. The moment that turned into enough time for a kettle of water to evaporate and then the kettle to melt from the heat.

I could have killed everyone, Derek.

"It was an accident, Bass, no. You can't think like that."

Yes. I could have burned down the entire kitchen. The apartment. The entire building. The building next door. Miguel is too old to get out. The boys on the fourth floor would have been trapped. I don't even know if the fire escapes are safe. I could have killed everyone. I could have killed everyone because I forgot and I don't even remember wanting tea.

The confusion turned to grief, mourning the deaths that hadn't happened but could have. Could have. I could have killed everyone.

The tears returned and stuck in my throat.

I don't even remember. Even when I saw the misshapen plastic and the lonely mug and dry tea bag.

"You can throw away the kettle. We can get another one."

That's not the point.

"I'm worried, Bass. This isn't about the kettle."

※

IT'S ABOUT THE DISAPPOINTMENT that greets me most mornings. It's about the way the fog covers my entire body. It's about my memory and how it only exists in fragmented spaces. An acute and intense recalling of one particular hour or day. I remember the way the sky turned pink and purple after a rain in Oklahoma. I can smell the earth: damp and cleansed like someone had taken bleach to it. Other times, my memory is a broken mirror. I can make out an eye and what I think is the cut of a cheek, but there's a hole in the center of the forehead, negative space where an emotion should live. A question mark where there should be nothing but answers.

A kettle forgotten on a stove.

✳

WHAT'S WRONG WITH ME?

I folded myself into my lap, grief shooting like lasers from my body. I wanted to remember putting the kettle on. I needed fastidious, tidy Derek to tell me that I was lazy and careless and irresponsible. The smell of plastic lingered.

What's wrong with me? Slow rocking against the cabinet. What's wrong with me? Rocking against the cold marble of the kitchen floor. What's wrong with me?

"Nothing." Calm, patient Derek.

My brain was empty and full, all at once. The memories splintered and shifted until I could only assume that what was left was truth.

I know he knew the dents and cracks. He knew what to do when the anxiety turned kinetic and my body trembled under the weight of all the shifting.

"This isn't about the kettle," he said. "This isn't just about the kettle . . ."

I could hear the beginnings of fear in his voice, but in the pause I could picture patient, fastidious Derek pulling himself together. "I don't know what it is but whatever it is, we will figure it out . . . okay?"

Okay.

He asked me again if he should come down.

No.

He asked if I wanted to come up.

No. Maybe tomorrow.

The fog had suddenly lifted and left in its place a deathly calm. I was no longer trembling, but I still couldn't lift the confusion. It was quiet in my brain now. This is what happens. The storm. The quiet. The storm. The quiet. The storm.

I'm okay. I'm sorry I called you.

The quiet.

"Don't be sorry. Let's talk some more about what this could be."

The storm.

No. It's okay. I'm okay. Everything is fine.

Take Two for Pain

WAS AFRAID OF WHAT would happen.

There was an order to this thing. There was a disorder to this thing. There was a way to focus on staying quiet and being still when it became impossible to outrun. There was a way of not speaking too loudly and of mediating how quickly the words left my mouth. My life always felt as though it was coming undone, and I knew that rather than sink into this undoing, I had to fight it. And so I avoided anything that would erase the little control I had.

#

IN THE WALK-IN CLOSET in my parents' bedroom, there is a medium-sized Rubbermaid container. It's green and red and meant for Christmas decorations: bulbs, ornaments, lights, maybe even a wreath if you angled it a certain way.

The container could be a small pharmacy in a remote village—filled with everything from laxatives to vitamins to orange prescription bottles. It's where, growing up, I first saw something called Ambien and once, for a brief period when things were quiet in the house,

Prozac. But like the green and red Rubbermaid container, we never spoke about that silence. We tiptoed around the calm as we had once tiptoed around the rages. We whispered about not upsetting the new balance, while the green and red box upstairs sat filled with the answers to at least some of our questions.

⁜

WHEN I WAS STILL a body riddled with cracks but not yet split, I came home from Brooklyn for a weekend, hoping the familiarity would mend me. By this time my family had moved from the house where I'd grown up into another, bigger house with too many rooms. My room, once again, was in the basement.

One evening, when the bedroom felt too lonely, too far away from the rest of the world, I remembered the box. I knew it would still be in my parents' new bedroom upstairs, that it would still be green and red and hold no wreaths or ornaments. I found my way up the basement steps, past the kitchen with its makeshift medicine cabinet, past the empty family room, and up the stairs to the bedrooms. The house was quiet and empty, my family out continuing the lives they had created while I wasn't there.

The box was still the biggest thing in the closet, still out of place, not even hidden. I didn't know what I was looking for—something to make it stop, I suppose. I needed to dull it, to somehow sever the nerve endings.

I knew to avoid the laxatives. I had already done my battles with ballerina tea and syrup of ipecac. I searched for something that sounded like it would numb and dull. The first bottle read, "hypertension." The second said, "for pain." I tipped two into my open palm. They looked up at me like eyes of judgment. But there was nothing those eyes could say to me that mine hadn't already held.

The pills did what they were supposed to do—made me feel like I was floating away from myself. Made me feel like I couldn't feel. Made me nothing—easily blown by a slight breeze. Made me drift into the other, calmer, less lonely parts of myself.

⧽

THERE IS NO *THING* that happened, just a thing that sometimes happens. This is how your brain has learned to protect itself from you.

Just let it.

⧽

ALL MY LIFE, I feared being "bad." I already felt broken, already felt like there was something irreparably wrong with me, the least I could do was coat myself in "goodness": this idea that who we are is based on how we are seen; I followed the rules but now I wanted to feel something different—to feel better, to feel unbroken—more than I wanted anything else. I wanted something other than this Novocain and numbness. Its very name revealed its power: I wanted ecstasy.

The first time the pills found me was at a lounge in the West Village, bodies draped across each other on the red vinyl couches. I remember being mesmerized by someone's hair. It felt like the fur of a mythical creature. I couldn't stop running my fingers through it. And all the hands and skin were poured silk and all we wanted to do was touch and be touched. And there was no body finding a home inside me. There was no life doing its best to escape. There was warmth but no weight to remind me that I was still in a body that moved blood. I was made of magic and moonlight.

⧽

I MADE NEW RULES. Told myself they would keep me safe: I would isolate the experience, keep it away from my waking life—never with my regular friends. With my regular friends, I could still be the innocent who had trouble inhaling smoke, the one who gasped and insisted we leave when I spotted the table of powder at a private party in SoHo. They would never have to know about it. They would never have to know about me. In this way I convinced myself I would never become hooked, that it would never be part of my "real" life.

✳

PILLS FOUND ME ON the floor of a Bushwick apartment one night. It had all happened so quickly. One moment, I was a smiling, laughing, floating body, running my fingers up and down my arms—feeling as though every cell in my body was leaning into my touch. Like I was the most beautiful and the most quiet and the most peaceful and the most steady and the most joy-filled person in the room.

Then, just as quickly, the calm had turned frantic and frenetic, my body jerking like a live wire was running through me. I could feel my brain zap and spark. I could hear disembodied voices speaking over me, "She's tweaking." Heard them whisper to each other, "What should we do?"

But I was okay. I was going to die but it was okay. Death felt like a song. Like the soft hands rubbing warmth into my body. This was not what I had imagined but it was welcome.

"Come on, Bassey! Wake up."

I opened one eye and then the other and found them all in a circle, kneeling next to my apparently not dead body, smiling with relief. Ignoring my disappointment.

But I'm sure I died that night.

※

EVEN AFTER THAT NIGHT, I tried them again and again—hoping that each time would be the one that either cured me or broke me completely. The pills made me feel light and liquid like sunlight streaming through a window. I lived at the edge of this lightness, feeling like a prism, creating rainbows everywhere I touched.

I wanted to stay there forever, but eventually, inevitably, the crash would come. The light would turn dark and shadowed, the quiet bliss would turn chaotic. The fog would be thicker, denser—and still, no death.

※

THE PILLS FOUND ME at an apartment party in Manhattan, ecstasy delivering again, covering my despair with light cascading over my body and glitter and softness and tender sounds and I knew I could stay on it forever. The party spread to the roof and I was there, stumbling over to the ledge, watching the city glow and throw light at me. Every window, every building, every place that held a light felt like an offering to me. The stars were so close that I could reach out and grab them. I could keep their glow in my pocket. I climbed onto the roof's ledge and heard a scream. I turned to see the group of people below surge towards me.

"It's okay." I could feel the light spill from my mouth as I spoke: "It's okay. Everything is so beautiful." The roof ledge was thick and fine to stand on. It was steady. I was fine. "I just need to feel a star. Look how beautiful."

A friend walked towards me. "Hey, we can get you a star from inside."

"There are stars inside?"

"Yeah. A whole room full of them."

"I didn't see them."

There was a gasp as I swayed then, nearly losing my balance. What was wrong with everyone? I could see the gold and glitter falling out of my mouth. "It's okay. I have amazing balance. I used to have to stand for hours on one foot when I was bad. It's okay." I stood on my toes and did a slow deliberate turn. The gasps from the partygoers fell on me again. "What's wrong with y'all? Where's the music? Let's dance."

I had turned a full 180 degrees and lowered my head for the first time, turning my attention to the street below me. A stray cab lazily made its way down the street. There were heaps of trash on the corner. Suddenly the city was covered in dust. I stood there frozen—aware of the people on one side of me, ready to catch me or help me if I wanted to rejoin them, and the street on the other side, ready to catch me or help me if I needed to escape. This rooftop was far enough off the ground to support anybody who thought they could fly.

I could just go—the thought crossed my mind again and again, until suddenly I was a little less high and I turned away from the street, terrified of what it meant. I could finally sense that I wasn't okay. That I needed to get off the ledge, off the roof, away from these people I didn't recognize. "Help me down." The party sighed in relief as arms stronger than mine lifted me off the ledge to the roof deck. "I have to go."

"No, how about you lie down?" The voice attached to whoever was holding me up led me into the apartment.

"I'm fine. I can do it."

The couch was already littered with bodies so I found a bedroom and a floor. I must have slept because the next thing I remember was feeling the ecstasy leaving my body, replaced by fear and loneliness.

Disheveled and dirty, I took the train from the Lower East Side to Brooklyn. I made it from the train station to my apartment building as the sun struggled to rise. The crash continued until all I could feel was shame and dirt, no more gold and glitter. I always forgot that this was next—the clock would strike on the hour and the magic would deposit me in the street like Cinderella after the ball, torn and tattered, left with only memories that couldn't capture the light she'd possessed just a few hours before.

✳

THAT WAS THE LAST time I searched for myself in a purple pill. Some early sense of self-awareness in me knew I couldn't afford to feel that good, or risk the depth of that crash, again.

Like a War

WE ARE IN CHICAGO or Brooklyn.

His arm is an anchor tied to my chest. He wants me to drown in him. He's pulled me so tightly into him that we no longer spoon. We are jackknife and pliers. His breath irritates the skin on the back of my neck. He's breathing in a staggered rhythm, like he's afraid every breath will refuse his lungs. Like he's gasping, or choking, but I'm the one who's drowning.

I'm awake. I'm always awake. I was awake in Hartford and Stillwater and St. Louis. I wanted my own hotel room. It was part of the contract. But I could feel his disappointment; he slumped against the wall when I suggested I enter it alone before the show.

"It's okay," I told him. "It's okay. I can just stay with you. We can be together. It's okay." So, I remained awake in Hartford and Stillwater and St. Louis and the hotel in Times Square after we taped the show.

I'm awake. I can tell by the way he's holding me that he's awake too, but I don't want to talk to him. I don't want any more tender, loving moments. I haven't slept in days and I don't want his arm across my body or his legs folded into the back of my knees or his breath on my neck. I want to sleep. I try to keep my body still, but not stiff. If I move too much, it will be a conversation in the morning. And I don't want to talk.

I want to sleep.

He pleads with me, his eyes the color of cornflowers and robins' eggs. He is so delicate. And hairy. And soft and bone. Always asking me to talk to him about my feelings. He says, "Tell me what you're feeling," but what he means is "Tell me how you feel about me. Tell me it hasn't changed." He smells like patchouli and patience.

Loving him is too much work.

We are in Brooklyn or Chicago.

We spent the day shopping and eating. Something vegetarian on West Fourth. I was running out of reasons why I loved him.

I told him that I needed to sleep. That there couldn't be another night of me stiff and still and breathing. I didn't tell him that I can feel every hair on his body when we sleep together. That I have come to hate the way he sweats when we fuck. We have started to fuck. I have started to pray that he will fuck me like he hates me. Like I am nothing. Like I am not the only reason he exists. Like I'm not responsible for his everything. I don't want to make love or have sex. I want to feel his heavy and thick and sweaty pressing me into the bed. He is always trying to please me, so I always try to be pleased. "You okay? Is this okay?" *It's okay. It's fine. I'm fine. Just lie on top of me. Just put your weight on me. Just let me feel that I'm not made of air and sadness.* But he wants to make love and his back is too hairy.

Too thick. Too sweaty. And I just want to fuck. I just want to feel his weight on me. I just want to bury myself into his shoulder and fall through the bed, through the floor, through the apartment, through the cement, through the grass and mud and dirt, into the center of the earth and burn there.

We are in Brooklyn or Chicago.

Probably somewhere else, somewhere that required a plane. He is afraid to fly, so he takes a Valium and clings to me on long flights. I have to hold him up. Soothe his fears even as he doesn't notice me slipping into nothing. I have to be brick and bone for him.

We are in Brooklyn or Chicago.

We went to the health food store earlier that day and rummaged the shelves, searching for something herbal and easy to encourage sleep. He wanted to be the only thing I needed. "Maybe if I gave you a massage," he suggested, "or bathed you. Or washed your hair. Or maybe if I read to you softly. Or if I held you."

He is always holding me. It isn't enough. I need more than him. He needs too much of me.

We are in Brooklyn or Chicago.

He hates when I dress up. "I like you natural," he says. He wants me bare-faced and shell-toe sneakers and sweatpants. He said he can't find me underneath all the makeup even though I only wear powder and lipstick; he makes it sound like I'm wearing a mask. What he really means is that he hates my made-up lips. He hates how other people float down my face to the ripe fruit of my mouth. He hates the attention that isn't his.

To avoid the conversation, I've started to lean into him before I get dressed. Press my face against his and let his tongue find a home in my mouth. I can feel him deflate when I pull away. He makes me feel responsible for the times others have left him. But I still slide lipstick onto my mouth. I'm an artist, meticulous in my application. Powder so it holds. Liner to prevent bleeding. The careful glide of color across the curve of top lip, then the plump and full of bottom. Mouths are important to me. I need them on myself and others to stay present. Staring into someone's eyes makes me squirm with discomfort or dishonesty. They say not making eye contact is how you know not to trust someone. But this isn't about that. If I don't focus on moving mouths, then I disappear. Mouths help me remain.

After I'm dressed, I make sure he doesn't kiss my mouth. Offer him a cheek or a hand. I can feel him looking at me out of the corner of his eyes. He is always looking at me. Always touching me. Always making me aware of my body and flesh. Always reminding me that I am there when he means to remind just himself. I don't need the reminders.

I was here.

I am here.

I will be here.

It makes me hate him and long for him at the same time.

I'm in Brooklyn. He's in Chicago. We are apart for just one week. We are in Boston.

Before the road trip, he surprises me with the *Chicago* soundtrack. A few days before that, he sent a bouquet of white roses to my apartment for Valentine's Day. He remembered the story I told about never receiving a "secret-admirer" carnation for Valentine's Day in high school. The note read: "These aren't carnations, but I hope they will do. I love you. Your Secret Admirer."

He's thoughtful. He's kind. It's not him, it's me. I want to be a good girlfriend. I want to find joy in these things he does. But I've been too tired to be affectionate. In Boston, I plan to surprise him. I am self-conscious about the red lingerie I have hidden in my suitcase. We go to a show together. We have dinner in the quaint bed-and-breakfast. I slip away from him and prepare. I want him to walk in and find me ready for him on the bed. But I don't feel sexy. I feel awkward. I feel broken. I feel tired.

When he returns to the room, I am in a T-shirt and pajama pants. He wants to hold me. I let him. I let him. I let him, but I'm not there. I'm in the bathroom looking at myself in red lace and thinking about how my body blooms and shrinks in all the wrong places, wondering if dinner was a mistake. I'm in the bed shifting my weight so his hand leaves my waist and lands on my back.

"I love you," I tell him when he cups my face. I'm ashamed at how his face glows when I say it. Has it been that long? Have I been that cruel?

"I love you too," he whispers as he places his forehead on mine. "I love you so much."

This is when it's good. I try my best to stay in the moment, in the room with him.

In the morning, I hold his hand with both of mine while he checks out. I'm holding on so I know we are both real. He turns to me and smiles, kisses me on the forehead, then places his cheek on top of my head. I don't remember being this much shorter than him. *Am I shrinking? Am I getting smaller? Am I disappearing?*

I shrug away from him, suddenly uncomfortable. His smile fades. I want to tell him I love him, but I left myself with the lingerie in the room upstairs.

We are in Brooklyn or Chicago.

I want to sleep. I've taken the melatonin and have promised him a movie and time spent. We are together all the time, but we are never together enough for him. I want to tell him that I can't breathe, but I'm never sure if it's because of him or because of me or because of me or because of me. Because I can't breathe, and I can't sleep, and he wants to be the only thing I need, and he isn't.

So, I leave him in the living room. I need a few moments not to be a home for him. I change out of my jeans and shirt and slide into a T-shirt, likely his. As I change, as I sit on the bed, I start to feel a buzz in my head. Something heavy begins to tug at my eyelids and then at my body. I know I should head back to the couch to fold into him, wait for sleep to come, but it's been so long since I've been sleepy and not merely tired, that I lean back onto the pillow instead. I want to enjoy the lightness of this moment, the impending sleep, the way it allows my body to fall into a haphazard rest. I remember floating.

We are in Brooklyn or Chicago.

He's naked. I'm never naked. Even at my fittest, I feel more comfortable in clothes. I need to feel like I can run at any moment. And naked means a scramble for clothes and shoes and not enough time to do both.

I can see the kitchen from the bed in his one-room studio. It is Chicago cold outside but he is naked and unwrapping a frozen pizza. We have just come from the movie *Antwone Fisher*. I could feel him looking at me from time to time in the theater. Each time I felt his head turn, I squeezed his hand. I wanted to let him know that I saw him; that I loved him despite not knowing what to do with him or what it meant.

Watching him, he seemed less hairy. Less heavy. His ass curves a bit more. The way he stands is the same though, shoulders always slightly hunched, as if he's ducking underneath a doorway or bowing to a silence. He turns to me and sees me watching him and smiles. I remember that I love him.

Later, we are at the table. He likes to thank me for dining with him. It was cute the first few times, but after months, it became tiresome. Like he was performing. No. Like he was auditioning. I am already there. I don't know what more he wants from me.

I am already there.

We are in Brooklyn or Chicago.

The pillow is soft against my head. I'm thinking about an open field and running. No. I'm not thinking. I'm dreaming. This is a dream. This is sleep. It has been days and I could feel the way my body melted into the dreaming. Like a sigh. Like a well-choreographed greeting. Me and the field and the dreaming. My body finally resting. But then there is a shaking. Someone calling my name. Shaking me. Shaking me. Waking me. The field is starting to slip away. I'm no longer running. I'm in Brooklyn. Awake again.

He's leaning over me with tears in his eyes. "You fell asleep without saying good night."

We are in Brooklyn or Chicago.

I used to like sex in the morning and in the middle of the day. I pulled him away from work with the innocent suggestions of naps. I pulled at him when my eyes opened and sun streamed through the windows. I pulled at him when he was already on top of me. In the beginning, we were all daytime sex and cuddles. But as the months went on, I started to disappear. Now there are no mornings for morning sex. No desire to lift my body towards him.

He thinks I'm leaving him because I no longer want him inside me. He doesn't see that I don't exist. I'm disappearing. I don't want anything. Not food. Not him. Not even sleep—or rather sleep doesn't want me. Either way. I've become nothing and nothing needs nothing.

We are in Chicago.

My best friend, Tosin, is engaged. We were together on the small bed in his apartment when I got the call. It made us search for hope in each other. We spoke abstractly about the possibility of us. One day. Maybe. He doesn't know that I don't believe in the future any more. But I do love him; he makes me think that I can begin to believe again.

We watch *The Sound of Music* because he knows it makes me happy. He so desperately wishes he could make me happy.

We are in Brooklyn or Chicago.

He's crying. Again. It must have been something I said. I stare at this face that I love and hate, willing my hand to reach out and stroke his cheek. Willing my mouth to try to explain this chaos that is consuming me. I must stare too long, let too much silence swell around us.

"What?" he asks, that constant nervousness in his voice making his vowels quiver so that it comes out as "Whaaaat?"

My love turns irritant and rises to my throat. I want to scream, to throw things at him. To ask him why I always have to take care of him without him ever noticing that I need saving too. His eyes widen, my silence fueling the anxiety flickering, creating a tic in his right eyebrow. His tooth, the one in front slightly longer than its neighbor, seems to grow until it looks like a lonely saber tooth. I blink twice to erase the image. I must stare at him too long because he comes towards me and takes my hand, his shaking still. I let his hands consume mine.

"What?" he asks again, his eyes welling up.

"Nothing. You want to take a nap?"

He smiles, relieved that it hasn't become a breakup or an argument or anything that would require him to be rock against my tidal wave. This time I welcome his arm across my body. This time the tickle of his beard on my bare back is a warming. I have to protect us from my instability.

We are in Dallas.

He is always afraid that he's going to lose me. He searches for me in crowds when we're the only two in the room. Searches in the dark at night. I start to wonder if he can even see me. *Do I exist? Why is he always looking for me?*

He is always afraid he's going to lose me. I smile at the waiter too long. Linger with the salesman. Blush at his friend's smile. I'm always convincing him that I'm not leaving until I do.

When we are together, he notices that I watch women as they pass us. I'm trying to figure out how they own their bodies like that. How they can exist in the world so fully and clearly while I feel like I'm fading into any background. Can they see me? I need to see myself.

One night, in Chicago, after he has buried his face between my legs, he slides up and kisses me before my body has even stopped its quivering. I want to inhale him. To find the proof that I'm real on his lips. I'm grateful for the reminder. It feels like a gift. I want to thank him. The words haven't fully formed in my throat when he asks, "Is that it? Is that why you've been so distant?"

I haven't heard him. Haven't realized he's been speaking. "What?" I ask, trying to find his eyes in the dark of the room.

"Are you a lesbian?"

"Are you serious? Why would you even ask me that?"

"I see how you watch them. How your eyes trail their asses as they pass."

I push him off me.

"I'm sorry," he says, as I walk out of the room. "I'm sorry," he says, as I fold myself into the couch. "I'm sorry," he says, kneeling before me. I stare at him. "I'm sorry." This time a whisper. I can hear his voice tremble.

I want to crack a joke, turn his fear into something we can laugh about later. I want him to save me, to fix me. I want to ask him to dance with me, to walk with me, to sit at the basketball courts down the block from his apartment. I want to reach up and wrap my arms around his neck, pull him on top of me. I crave the weight of his body crushing me instead of his questions, but before I can move or breathe or utter a word he says, "You didn't answer the question."

I pull my body back and disappear into my mind.

I remember that I hate him.

We are in Brooklyn or Chicago.

I had been asleep when he woke me to complain that I hadn't tended to him before I had eased into my own comfort. He said I had forgotten him, and now I am angry. I haven't slept for days and he's watched me fight and plead and cry for my own safe place to land. And then he woke me. Because I had forgotten him in the living room.

"Why couldn't you just let me sleep?" I scream.

He is on the floor now, his body a tight ball, and he is wailing. I want to hit him for being weak, for turning me into my mother. I want to fly at him with my fists and my feet and my mouth. But all I can do is scream, "Get out! Get out! Get out of my house!"

He's asking me where he should go. Suddenly he's sorry. Reaches for me. Grabs my face and tries to point my mouth towards his. Towards him. He's searching for my mouth. I don't know where my roommate is. But I am screaming for him to leave. "Get out!"

"But it's my birthday," he says, his voice quivering. I can see the tears creating pools of glass in his eyes.

"Get out!"

"But I don't have anywhere to go."

"Get out!"

"We're in Brooklyn. Where can I go?"

I say nothing. To open my mouth would be to invite more acid-soaked anger or worse, an invitation to forget it all and reconcile. I watch him gather his bag. He wants me to stop him. To leap into his arms like in the romantic comedies he hates that I love. I don't watch him leave. I turn my body to the wall, offer my back.

He doesn't leave, only moves to the couch.

Morning comes, he enters and lifts the sheets, ready to offer his body as an act of contrition. I stare past him. He's waiting for me to pull him into my arms and on top of me; ask him if he wants to take a nap. I close my eyes, shut him out instead.

This silence is like a war.

This time, he leaves. He's gone to see a friend. I know he's telling them how crazy I am. How he tries his best and all I offer is cruelty.

I'm awful. He will tell them that he loves me. I expect a call pleading on his behalf.

Later that night, things are calmer. I ask him to return.

He is in the living room making awkward conversation with my roommate. When it's time to talk, in the bedroom, I apologize for the night before. I want to apologize for all the nights and the days when I am filled with rage, for being a person who can't seem to make sense. I want to tell him about how it feels to need comfort and quiet and have to push it aside to quiet and comfort him. He doesn't understand. Asks me over and over if I'm breaking up with him. Tells me over and over that he can fix it. He doesn't understand. My roommate is in the other room watching the Oscars. She calls for me, "Hey, Bassey, get out here! It's your guy on TV." The actor from *Y Tu Mamá También*. Her way of saving me. Of giving us the space we are too crushed to take. When she sees me, she gives me a sympathetic smile. The smile says: Stay here for a bit. Cool off. Wait before you say more things you don't mean.

I take a moment with her to laugh about how cute the actor is, comment that his English is getting better. I know I can't stand there for much longer, but I'm calmer. I'm ready to talk. I'm open.

He's not. He's sitting on my bed, his head in his hands. Looks up when I reenter.

"Really?" he says. "You're going to walk out in the middle of an argument because some dude you like is on TV?"

"That's not why . . ."

"Then why? You're hurting me," he says.

I begin to laugh.

"I'm *hurting* you, really?" I laugh in his face. "Oh you poor thing. You want me to make you feel better?" I mock him for his softness; call him pathetic.

He sits on the bed, shocked, and stares at me like he's never seen me before. I want him to fight with me. I want to hit him. I want him to hit me. I want him to yell and scream with me. I want him to fight me. But he just sits and stares, and then quietly, "You're mean," he says. "You're mean."

The truth of that settles in the space between us and I flinch with shame.

I am mean. I'm also dying in front of him and he doesn't see me.

This has to end. It has to be over.

He doesn't want us to end. Says, "Maybe we just need some space. Maybe we need to remember ourselves without each other." Me in Brooklyn. He in Chicago. I agree to this. We promise that we will one day be vegan hot dogs in Gramercy Park again. I want to believe that—believe in something. I need a moment to find life within me again. It's not him. It's me. The cliché with some truth in it. We just need a break. We love each other—I think. But I know how my brain works. How easily it folds, losing people in the crease. I know I love him—I think, but I'm tired. Always.

⧣

IT'S MONTHS LATER, OUR communication has been sporadic: tense emails, I call him from Edinburgh, he sends me books with handwritten letters trapped in pages. We have yet to return to vegan hot dogs, but I need his hope, I need the way he sees me. I am existing as ash. I cover everything I touch in soot. I have carried my body across these cities and across the ocean for this tour. I am now in Atlanta.

He tells me in a short email that he will be there at the same time, has his own show somewhere else. He agrees to see me. I want to see him, try to remember the last time I felt like a person who could be touched and loved.

I felt like a ghost haunting the world, trying to find rest.

"You look different," my voice shakes.

"I go to the gym now."

He is different: His beard is thick and untamed, like when we first met; it is no longer the precisely cut goatee that I told him I prefer. His arms are bigger, more toned. I reach for him. His hug is quick, creating space rather than closing distance. He's different. He is rock and steady and brick-wall. He's come prepared to fight against whatever siren song I sent him.

We must talk. I don't know what about. I don't know how long he's there, but I know that I beg him to stay.

"Stay with me.

"This place is huge and probably nicer than your hotel.

"Stay with me . . .

"Let's take a nap."

Stay with me.

Stay with me.

Stay with me.

Save me.

Save me.

Save me.

But he is rock and steady and brick-wall. He refuses my face and my mouth, pushes my body away from his.

"You hurt me. Why do you want me now? I can't."

He belongs to someone else. I can tell.

"Already? You're with someone new already?" I scan my memory for hints in his letters or emails or background voices in that call from Edinburgh. I should have known; there is always someone new. He had to be sure of me before he left the one before me. There's always someone new for him.

He says nothing. I am a ball on the floor. I am wailing.

"Get out! Get out!"

He doesn't move towards me; makes no attempt to comfort. He steps back. He turns. I'm screaming for him to come back. *Stay with me. Stay with me. Save me. Save me. Please.* He slips out. Doesn't answer my calls. And I call and call and call. I do what I do every night: I pull myself off the floor and find my way onstage for a few hours. After the show, instead of returning to my room, I go to the hotel bar. I need to drink until my mind belongs to me again. This makes sense somehow. Another. Another. Another. Another. Another. I call him again and again and again. I sing into the phone. I am a terrible singer. He doesn't return my calls. He has someone else to hold. Found her not long after our last goodbye. He needs someone. Someone who will stay. Someone who is the opposite of me. White like him. Someone his mother would like. Someone kinder. Someone not broken. Someone not mean.

He's gone. And I am here. Crumbling against the weight of whatever is trying to kill me. It's winning. I am tired of fighting.

And nobody can save me.

This Is What Happens

11:40 A.M.

IT'S NOT SO MUCH the traveling.

It's the airplanes and the airports and the security screenings. The TSA agents and the bored way they ask, "Miss, please put your belongings in the bin" and "Please step to the side and wait for assistance." I hate waiting for flights that are delayed and missing those that come in on time. I hate flight attendants and their tiny useless bags of pretzels. I hate preparing for takeoff and landing and the baby four rows back that will not stop crying. I hate the man next to me, who insists on both the seat by the window and a conversation. I hate myself for not telling him that I need a place to rest and have no room for company. But his voice is better than mine. So, I listen.

12:00 P.M.

I am flying home. In three hours, I will be in New York, but in less than twenty-four there will be another airplane, another airport, another city.

2:42 P.M.

The plane lands exactly ten minutes ahead of schedule, but the doors remain locked. "Ladies and gentlemen, we apologize for the delay. We're just waiting for clearance before we open the doors, please be patient." The captain has assured us that it will only be a "short while longer" at least eight times. I stopped counting when I became overwhelmed by the fear that we'd be asked to take our seats again, fasten our seat belts, and then be flown somewhere further from home than Brooklyn feels.

2:44 P.M.

There is something forming in my throat. It has become more and more familiar these last weeks. I am tired of it. It's an always wanting to cry, it's the almost crying and it's the barely keeping it together because there is a small girl, white socks and first plane ride, across the aisle from me.

2:45 P.M.

I've learned to stare at my shoes until they become blurry and liquid.

3:15 P.M.

The doors have finally opened. I grab the bags stashed under the seat in front of me.

I want to run, push, and bump my way past the people in the aisle. But I steady myself, wait for others to pass. Smile. "No. Go ahead. It's fine." I've practiced that as well. I grab my carry-on from overhead and ease my way down the rows of empty seats—all upright and in their full and locked positions. Manage a "thank you" to the flight attendants who will forget me before I pass them.

3:17 P.M.

There are no new messages on my cell phone.

3:20 P.M.

I don't expect any anxious faces at baggage claim, but I still search and scan the signs for my name.

3:30 P.M.

I grip the handle of my bag tight and pull, half walking, half running to the nearest exit. The wind hits my face and I breathe for the first time in days. Perfect. I'm right in front of the taxi stand. *Damn!* I forgot to look for an ATM. The idea of going back into the airport makes my throat swell again. I check my wallet and find $27 and a mountain of change. I can't remember what it takes to get to Brooklyn.

3:34 P.M.

The queue at the taxi stand is shorter than I expect. It's colder in New York than I remember. I am tired.

3:45 P.M.

It's my turn. The attendant hands me the folded yellow paper covered in taxi-cab law that is meant to protect tourists. Usually, I shrug them off, announce, "I live here." Today, I'm not sure where I belong. The driver lifts himself from the front seat and offers to put my bags in the trunk.

"No. I'm fine. I'll hold them." I climb into the back and clutch everything to my chest.

"Where you go, miss?"

"I don't know."

"Pardon?"

"Sorry. Brooklyn. Flatbush to Eastern Parkway. I'll direct you from there."

"What's the exact address, miss? I know the area."

I tell him off Nostrand.

"I know the area, miss. I live very close by."

I nod. The thoughts have started to flood. They tumble and race so quickly that only focusing on him helps slow their circling. I can't stop nodding. I want to start a conversation, make him talk to me. I open my mouth slightly but I'm not sure where to start. I bite my bottom lip and say nothing. I think that maybe he will wonder about me and I wait. No. He's done with me, concentrating only on navigating his cab out of the airport. I realize that I am tense and leaning forward so I push back and stare at my shoes.

3:48 P.M.
The silence is as thick as the plastic that divides us.

4:00 P.M.
The cab is too hot, so I crack the window. Let November enter.

"Miss, which way you wanna go?" His voice cuts through the air.

I lean forward. "Um . . . I-I don't know. Wherever, I mean, I don't, I don't—care. Whatever you think is best."

I can't seem to focus on his question or my answer. I open my mouth to clarify but he—

"Okay. Too much traffic here so I take you the fast way. BQE."

—understood.

I nod and fall back into the seat again. As I stare outside, the view rises and falls in a blur of shapes and colors. The arc and speed invite car sickness so I face forward. The ID on the glass shows a small, brown man, smiling for an unknown photographer. His name is Hasaan. Hasaan. I've always liked the name Hasaan. I like how the *a*'s are the only vowels.

4:15 P.M.

We drive from Queens to Brooklyn in silence, but my mind is never quiet: yesterday, tomorrow, last night, tomorrow night, the next city, the last city, the next show, the last show, when will this end, need sleep, don't want food, don't want sleep, need food, sleep, sleep, sleep, sleep. I sigh and shake my head to clear the chatter. Hasaan looks at me through the rearview mirror. *Smile. Invite him to talk.* I need his voice as solid rock against the dust crumbling around me. But I can't manage a smile and look away instead. All I have of him is his name. That's all I need. I murmur it, under my breath, over and over, "Hasaan. Haasaaan. Hasaaan. Haaasaaaan." His name becomes a mantra reminding me to breathe. I can feel something start but I push it to the base of my throat. I stare at this forgotten, folded yellow paper. I find Brooklyn on the small map. Home.

4:18 P.M.

I can feel fatigue eating through my bones.

4:30 P.M.

"Miss, this is good, yes?"

I look up to find Hasaan facing me. It takes a moment to realize that the cab has stopped and pulled up to a curb.

4:31 P.M.

I sit in the cab and stare out into the street. I'm not sure what I'm waiting for. Hasaan clears his throat from the front seat.

"Miss, if you please . . ." I nod, for what seems like the millionth time. Then I pull out my wallet and hand him all the bills. I don't wait for change or a receipt or even to see if I've given him enough. I just throw my body against the door, praying that it will open. I drag my bags after me. I stand on the curb, wallet in hand, trying to suppress an urge to run. Flatbush pulsates around me. There are several radios full blast, all battling each other for control of the street noise. There's a mess of Rasta men outside a repair shop and old women in front of the 99-cent store trying to keep warm while waiting for the B44 bus. Right then, I decide I want to be someplace else—anywhere but here. I turn back toward the street just in time to see the stoplight is now green, the last bit of yellow disappearing around the corner. He's gone. I stare at my shoes and swallow. I stand on the sidewalk and face the apartment building.

There is the faint smell of burning hair in the air and rapid Spanglish spilling onto the street from the Dominican beauty salon at the end of the block. Next to it is a window filled with plastic flowers and many glowing statues of the Virgin Mother. Across the street is the bodega. Inside it smells like wet dog and hot breath. The owner always greets me with "Aye, mamita!" when I enter through the door. He always seems glad to see me. I wonder, briefly, if I should take my bags and head to his store first, but I think better of it.

5:00 P.M.

I turn away from the bodega with a sigh and face my building. To the right, underneath a dirty white something that barely remembers when it was an awning, is a man the color of sand. He has thick arms and a belly that balloons over his belt buckle. I think he is the owner and has come out to guard his wares. I'm not sure what he's protecting. He sells nothing but headboards shaped like swans and statues of naked women dancing and shining in black lacquer. He sits in a wicker rocking chair and moves lazily back and forth; cradling a ceramic mermaid-shaped lamp. This lamp he holds like his firstborn is the ugliest, most beautiful thing I have ever seen. And at this moment, I have never wanted anything more. I want to cradle it like he does, trace my fingers along the ridges and then smash it. I want to own something ugly and destroy it. I am fixated on the lamp, staring at it like it will spring to life.

"You lost or something like that?" Mr. Furniture's booming voice forces me to look up.

I shake my head no.

He struggles to stand. He and his mermaid lamp take a few steps towards me.

"You all right there?" he asks suspiciously, clutching the lamp to his heaving chest. "You stand there a long time."

"I live here. I'm just looking for my keys."

I open my purse and begin searching earnestly. I pull them out and jiggle them before heading towards the door. I make a big production of sliding the key into the lock. I turn the knob praying that this is not one of the times it sticks. I push the door open with as much dramatics as I can manage. I turn to face the man and his lamp and give him a smirk.

Satisfied, Mr. Furniture turns and, with a slight juggling of the lamp, shuffles back to his store. Like anyone would want to steal his tacky-ass furniture.

5:08 P.M.
The corridor is as dark and dank as ever. I'm not sure if these legs will remember three flights of stairs.

5:10 P.M.
They do, but barely.

5:13 P.M.
I leave my bags by the front door. There is never a reason to unpack. The first thing I do is pick up a remote control—I don't care which one. I need the noise. I press power. The stereo starts with the familiar click and shhh of a turning CD. With another click, the quiet is abruptly ended. The music fills in the empty spaces.

5:14 P.M.
The apartment is empty and immaculate. My roommate likes to clean before she leaves town so there's a shine and a neat to everything. It all looks so different. I wander around like I'm in a museum, too afraid to touch anything. I don't want to disturb the order.

5:25 P.M.
The bathroom is small and easy. I spot the new shower curtain immediately. The bath mat is now blue—or was it always blue?

5:35 P.M.
The kitchen is exactly the same. The microwave still owns the counter across from the stove. In the cabinet—peanut butter and a can of Goya peas we are sure came with the apartment. This is good. Some things are still familiar.

5:43 P.M.

My bedroom is exactly as I left it—a complete mess. Between books and half-filled journals, there is, also, an avalanche of clothes on the floor and overflowing from the dresser. My closet is over-stuffed. The clothes still on the closet rod are hanging on for dear life. Below the clothes are my shoes, all thrown together, scuffed and mismatched and upside down. Only a few of the newer ones are safe, awkwardly stacked in their boxes.

I really should treat my things better.

5:44 P.M.

I'm reaching to pick up a stray T-shirt when I see the laptop. Sleek and silver, sitting abandoned and angry on my nightstand, a sock draped mockingly over it. This is my most prized possession. My first major purchase—well, sort of. At the last minute, I had to put it on my roommate's credit card. But with this job, I paid her back in a week.

5:45 P.M.

The realization hits that this job bought most of the new and expensive things scattered around the room. I don't have to worry about bills or rent or my out of control eBay habit because of this job. This job that I'm so lucky to have, this job that I am constantly reminded not to take for granted, this job that people would die for. I'm waiting for it to kill me.

6:00 P.M.

I'm tired. I need sleep but it has become such a challenge. I wonder if I've forgotten how. I look at my bed now, crumpled and untidy. It's so strange to know hotel beds so well that I forget the look and feel of my own. *Maybe if you make your bed.* I nod. *Yes. Maybe.* I look at the mess and search the debris for promises.

6:15 P.M.

I can't remember the last time my bed was made. The sheets smell new and crisp. I remember reading somewhere that white is soothing. That it's the color of peace. I'm pretty sure this is bullshit, but anything is worth a shot. I stand and stare at my bed. Its tidiness makes sleep even more unappealing.

6:20 P.M.

I should shower; remove this layer of travel and hurry from my body.

6:22 P.M.

My jeans slide off without first unbuttoning or unzipping.

6:30 P.M.

I sit on my bed. I've forgotten what I undressed for.

6:42 P.M.

In the blue and white bathroom, the water in the tub is running. All I need is a shower. After this everything will make more sense.

6:45 P.M.

The hot water is taking its time. I sit at the edge of the tub, feeling the temperature struggling to change under my fingers. My stomach rumbles a little and I try to recall my last meal. Last night in the hotel. We were in Atlanta for three days. For every meal there, I ordered room service: the fruit plate (no melon, yes that includes cantaloupe but extra watermelon if you have it) and a pitcher of water (no ice) and a glass of ice (no water, please). The same room service guy brought in the tray each time. He'd laugh and say, "Be careful or you'll turn into a pineapple." In every hotel, in every city, every room service worker tells the same joke.

6:57 P.M.

I put my hand under the tap and then pull it away as the water changes suddenly from lukewarm to hot hot. I turn the knob and try to adjust the stream pelting the plastic shower curtain. I can smell the heat as the temperature in the shower changes. I pull the tucked ends of my towel free and drop it on the floor. *You should really treat your things better.* When I bend over to pick it up, I catch a glimpse of myself in the mirror. I move away quickly but not before seeing skin pulled tight along a poking collarbone. I resist the urge to look again and step gingerly into the shower.

7:00 P.M.

The bathroom is clouded by steam. I watch as it fills the room and covers the mirror. I pull the curtain closed.

I want to own something ugly and destroy it.

8:17 P.M.

I stay in as long as I can. Wash every part of my body more than once. The spaces between my toes, the curves behind my ears have never been so clean. When there is nothing left to scrub raw, I sit at the bottom of the tub and let the water beat me.

8:20 P.M.

I need to get out before I drown. I wonder if I could drown? It would be an accident.

8:25 P.M.

I manage to drag myself out. I miss the pounding of the water already. I briefly consider taking another shower. I can feel fatigue eating through my bones.

8:27 P.M.

There is something familiar rising. I've learned its pattern. It starts at the back of my neck, tightens and spreads to the space between my shoulders. In less than a second, it will hit me squarely in the chest, take my breath, rush my heartbeat, turn my knees to water. I don't have time for it now. I'll just have to shake it off; try to steady myself. There's nothing wrong with me. I'm only tired. I only need to sleep or eat. I will not shiver and shake with it.

8:30 P.M.

This thing disappears as quickly as it appeared.

8:31 P.M.

I sit on the edge of the bathtub and stare at my feet; waiting for it to come back.

8:32 P.M.

I don't know what's wrong with me.

8:35 P.M.

I feel a chill and remember the cooling bathroom and reach for my towel.

8:38 P.M.

In my bedroom, I dig through layer after layer of pants and shorts and sweatshirts for something to wear—none of them will prevent the thing should it chose to come back. *The pink flannel won't help you. The eighth-grade gym shorts won't encourage you to eat. The gray fleece won't invite sleep.* I shake my head to stop the words. I need my black Old Navy sweatpants. They will make this place feel like home. They are oversized and soft and fading. I search through T-shirts and bras and tank tops and towels. I cannot find them in this mess I've created.

8:40 P.M.

I sit on the floor. I can feel the thing again. This time I don't stop it. The frustration is too much. *How many times has your face been wet the last few weeks? How often have you tasted the salt? When was the last night you weren't huddled on a floor?*

I hold my head and sob until my stomach aches.

8:43 P.M.

The floor feels like concrete through the thin terry cloth. I curl myself into a ball, feel my face cool against the hardwood. I cannot convince my body that I am worth rising for. *This doesn't happen to normal people.* I close my eyes tighter and pull my knees closer to my chest. I try to think of Hasaan. I want to stay like this forever.

9:00 P.M.

But I can't stay here.

9:05 P.M.

I finally sit up, dizzy, and try to regain control of my breathing. *This doesn't happen to normal people.*

9:07 P.M.

My body is unforgiving. I have been moving slowly through these cotton and molasses days, getting by on just enough. Just enough sleep. Just enough air. Just enough food. Just enough rest. Just nearly not enough. *How much longer can you do this?* I'm waiting for it to kill me.

9:10 P.M.

My heart jumps as the CD ends suddenly. I sit on the floor, legs folded. I scan the room searching for something. I need other voices. I remember my cell phone in the other room and mentally scan the names inside for someone I can call. There is no one. No one who will ignore that it's been weeks, sometimes months since the last time we spoke. There is too much to explain. I've lost touch. *You're a terrible friend. No wonder you're alone.*

9:20 P.M.

I've been trembling and convince myself that it's the cold. I stand up too quickly and the walls rush towards me. It takes a moment to steady myself.

My bedroom is so cluttered. The mess is overwhelming. All I can do is stand in the middle and wring my hands over and over and over.

9:25 P.M.

Fall is sliding in from the windows. I need to get dressed.

9:30 P.M.

I've picked through the pile of clothes near my dresser. I still can't find my sweatpants. The pink plaid pajama bottoms will have to do. I sit on my bed and look around. *You need to clean up.* I nod to myself. I put my feet up, hug my knees to my chest, and rest my forehead on my knees. I wish I could sleep like this.

9:45 P.M.

The comforter does little to live up to its name. It's too hot underneath, too cold on top. I've calmed down enough to lie still. I am a tight curl on my bed. I think it helps with the shivering. I can't move for fear the sobbing and trembling will return. I try my best to focus on one thing. I can't. I need to tell someone about this. But who? What? What is *this*? How can I tell someone when I don't even know what this is?

How could I possibly explain this to anyone? They'll only tell me to try and sleep and try and eat. As if it's that simple. As if that's the real problem.

Is this what crazy feels like? The question makes my heart quicken. My body is, again, a mess of tremble and panic. All I can think about is how I'm wearing the pink pajama bottoms. I need my black sweatpants. They are the only thing that feels good. I drag my luggage from the front door into the bedroom. I search, more determined than I've been in weeks. I've never learned to pack properly. There is so much to sift through. I will need to do laundry in the next city. I need to do laundry in this city. I suddenly remember the bag of laundry I didn't have time to send out the last time I was here. It's in the corner partially hidden behind the closet door.

10:20 P.M.
They are near the bottom.

10:21 P.M.
For the first time, in a long time, there is hope.

10:23 P.M.
I can sleep now.

11:00 P.M.
Still no sleep, but there is a bit of quiet. This thing, it comes in waves. I wait, grateful for this brief pocket of relief and terrified, anticipating the next explosion.

11:30 P.M.
It's too hot in here. I lift myself off the bed to open the window. I lean against the ledge and stare out at the late-night Flatbush traffic.

Nostrand Avenue is quieter than I remember. There are few people, even fewer cars, and a slight breeze. I stand there, looking out.

12:00 A.M.
I notice a woman trudging slowly underneath my window. She walks like there is something heavy pressing her into the pavement. I've seen her before. She is one of the many women who sit on the train at all hours of the day and night, sometimes surrounded by bags, sometimes an unopened book in their laps. If I look close enough, I can sometimes see the hint of the beauty and laughter they once held.

This thing could take you. *No,* I think to whoever controls these things, *I don't want to be like her.* The woman is ambling down the block, her walk a careful struggle. I want to call out to her, to run down those three flights and stop her. Beg her to tell me what happened. I want to know when she gave up, when all of this became too much to bear. I want to know if it started with a sleepless night, maybe two. Did it start with a tremble?

12:20 A.M.
I bite my lip and try to fight the thing wet and waiting behind my eyelids. But I don't move from the window. I just watch this woman until she turns the corner and disappears.

12:23 A.M.
I close the window and back away from it; afraid that the shaking will return. I need something: sleep or food.

12:25 A.M.
I need the television. Something that will help me forget.

12:30 A.M.

I sit in front of the television with the jar of peanut butter and a spoon. I grab the remote and power the television on. The room floods with sound, I allow myself a smile and a small sigh of relief. I scan past channel after channel. *Real World.* Click. *Rocket Chef.* Click. *Conan*Click*SouthPark*Click*ComicView*Click. I stop on a rerun of *Three's Company.* All I want is something familiar.

12:42 A.M.

My heartbeat is normal again.

12:43 A.M.

I'm still holding the peanut butter; trying to convince myself to eat. *Okay, whenever Jack falls, I'll take a spoonful.* A few moments later, John Ritter tumbles backwards off a couch. I unscrew the lid and dip my spoon in. The peanut butter is a chunky brown blob. I've never wanted anything less. I close my eyes and force a spoonful into my mouth. It is thick and heavy on my tongue. The bits of peanuts are like tiny pebbles. I almost can't bring myself to swallow. But I have to eat, even if it's just this. On the screen there is another fall, more canned laughter. I force another spoonful. Then I screw the lid back on the jar.

1:05 A.M.

I make it to the bathroom just in time. My stomach was already empty and the acid makes my throat burn. I sit against the bathtub, holding my head in my hands, waiting for the next wave to hit.

1:15 A.M.

I'm so tired that I can't sit still. I don't understand this. If I sit, I shake so much that I need to stand, and when I stand, I need to move until I'm tired, but no matter how tired I get I still can't sleep.

I'm walking quickly from one side of the apartment to the other. I have to keep moving. And my hands. I can only shake them, can only wring them. But never fast enough. Nothing is fast enough. Not the pacing. Nothing. Only the words dancing circles inside my head. The thoughts running and racing faster and faster. Until I'm begging for my skin to slide quickly off my bones. I spin around a few times, searching for something that will make this stop. Maybe I'll tire myself out. I'll have no choice but to collapse from exhaustion. Maybe my heart will explode from beating so fast. Maybe this time I won't wake up.

1:30 A.M.
Faith is a matter of interpretation. My belief in God has always been circumstantial. Disbelief requires too much proof. I don't have the time.

1:35 A.M.
So, for the next few minutes, I'll put everything I know into believing.

2:00 A.M.
And God accepts no bargains.

2:01 A.M.
I am on the floor again, this time holding my head and rocking. Back and forth and back and forth and back and forth. This is not helping.

2:09 A.M.
I'm waiting for this to kill me.

2:10 A.M.
I have to stand up—move. More pacing. More wringing of hands. More holding. The trembling will not stop.

2:15 A.M.
And God accepts no bargains.

2:30 A.M.
Bedroom. Living room. Kitchen. Living room. Bathroom. Bedroom.
Living room. Kitchen. Living room. Bathroom. Kitchen. Bedroom.
Kitchen. Bathroom. Living room. Bathroom. Kitchen. Bedroom.
Kitchen. Bedroom. Living room. Living room. Living room.

2:50 A.M.
I stand still and close my eyes. I start counting backwards from
2,000.

953. 952. 951.

It's working. Keep pacing. Keep counting.

493. 492. 491. 490. 489.

Keep counting. It's working.

3:00 A.M.
The shaking has lessened.

3:20 A.M.
I get to one but keep my eyes tightly shut. I'm afraid if I open them
it will all return.

3:31 A.M.
I wish I could sleep like this.

3:40 A.M.
You can't sleep now. You have a plane to catch in a few hours.

4:05 A.M.

I need water. Water always stays down. My body is both heavy and empty, but at least everything is quiet.

4:15 A.M.

My Adidas sports slippers are under the bed. They will have to do. I grab a coat from the closet. It is ankle-length, raspberry and wool. It is beautiful, not warm.

4:20 A.M.

I'm never sure about these stairs.

4:31 A.M.

The security guard looks up lazily as I enter, then returns to his magazine. The store is empty. There is only one cashier. She is sitting on the counter smoking a cigarette. She doesn't acknowledge me. I find the ATM and swipe my card.

4:34 A.M.
Password.

Withdrawal.

Checking.

$20.

Remember the car to the airport.

Cancel.

$60.

Enter.

No further transactions.

No receipt.

Have a Nice Day. *Thanks.*

4:40 A.M.
I head to the back where the refrigerators are. There are no gallons, only sports bottles. I grab two.

4:43 A.M.
As I stand there, the tubes and bottles start to blur and melt into each other. I close my eyes and shake my head.

4:45 A.M.
I need to get home.

4:50 A.M.
The cashier has finished her cigarette and is leaning on the counter. I can still smell the bitter and burn of tobacco and paper. When she sees me approach, she rolls her eyes and moves behind the register. I feel like I should apologize. My eyes begin to burn. I stare at my feet for a few seconds. Just to steady myself. When I look up, she is staring at me. She opens her mouth and words drift past me in slow motion.

I squint trying to read her lips. I try to stay focused on her face.

"Will. That. Be. All," she says again.

I want to tell her that I'm tired, not stupid.

You need to sleep.

"Yes. I mean, no . . ." The question tumbles out of my mouth before I can catch it: "Can you tell me where the sleeping pills are?" The words echo in my head.

You need them.

"I need to sleep." It takes me a minute to realize I've said this out loud.

The cashier gives me a look before she answers, "Aisle 4. Are you okay?"

I nod, afraid of what will come if I open my mouth again. I leave the bottles on the counter and turn around.

4:55 A.M.
Aisle 7.

Aisle 6.

Aisle 5.

Aisle 4.

4:57 A.M.
The shelves are filled with rows and rows of boxes. My eyes can't take them all in. I reach out and pick Tylenol PM. *If you take one, you won't get up in time.* I pick up another bottle. Nytol. *If you take one, you won't get up at all.*

I'm not sure what I'm looking for. All I know is that I want to sleep. *You're waiting for something to kill you.* I start to remember the hotel room in Dallas. The bottle—take two for pain. The eight pills I swallowed one after another. I remember my head pounding. Remember waking up on the bathroom floor, disappointment slapping me hard in the face. I told myself it was because of the headache that followed me into the morning. I remember the 4 train and the traffic on 14th and Broadway, the urge to jump great, the desire to be pushed greater still. But sleeping is allowed. *If you take one, you will take them all.* I'm just tired. *And alone.* And alone. *And lonely.* And lonely. I'm waiting for something to kill me. I'm waiting for sleep, maybe this time I won't wake up. All the things I haven't given myself permission to admit are pushing themselves past my filter and I'm hoping that this is a dream, that I did fall asleep all those hours ago on my bed. I can feel the tears making their way past my eyelids. I cover my mouth to stifle the cry. I don't know what to do so I sit in the middle of the aisle, holding the boxes to my chest. *You're supposed to know what to do.*

I don't know, tell me, what am I supposed to do . . .

5:10 A.M.
"Ma'am, are you all right?"

I look up to see the security guard. My head is spinning. "Yes. I'm fine. Thank you."

My voice has taken on an eerie, stilted calm. I'm aware of the security guard's eyes on me as I struggle to my feet. I'm not sure what to do with the boxes, so I set them on the shelf behind me.

I turn to the security guard and say, "I have a plane to catch in a few hours." He nods slowly and backs away from me. I wipe my face with my coat sleeve. I don't care if he doesn't believe me.

I am floating somewhere between bone and flesh.

5:15 A.M.

As I pass the register, the cashier reminds me of the water. I turn back and watch as she puts the bottles in a white plastic bag. She scans my CVS card and rings me up. I go through my wallet and find a 5-dollar bill. She gives me 23 cents. She hands me my receipt and asks again if I'm okay. I don't answer, just turn and leave.

5:16 A.M.

I'm not but this is the best I can do. I have a plane to catch.

5:17 A.M.

Outside, the sun has found time to rise. It's officially morning.

5:26 A.M.

These legs. Those stairs.

5:30 A.M.

I shed my coat at the door and make it to the bedroom. I sit and wait for this to kill me. I can't handle the weight of this.

5:31 A.M.

I lie back on the bed and stare at the ceiling.

5:35 A.M.

You need help.

I need to clean up.

5:42 A.M.

Maybe just lie here.

5:45 A.M.

Tell someone.

I should pack.

5:46 A.M.
Maybe just lie here.

5:52 A.M.
I shut my eyes. If I take one, I'll take them all.

"Stop it!" I scream, in this apartment that doesn't feel like my own. In the last few months, I have become familiar with the feel of hotels across the country. This place was supposed to help me sleep. It was supposed to be better here. It's not. I sit up and look around. *Find something ugly; destroy it.* I think of Mr. Furniture and his ugly, ugly, beautiful mermaid lamp. I want to own something ugly and destroy it.

5:55 A.M.
This hurts.

6:00 A.M.
I want to call someone. Tell them everything. But it's too early everywhere.

6:05 A.M.
I have a plane to catch. I need to pack.

6:20 A.M.
It will be another two weeks before I'm back.

7:10 A.M.
I've stuffed more clothes than I need back into my suitcase. I've cleared my bedroom the best I can in the little time I have. Everything is shoved in the closet or under the bed. I threw a few things

behind the wood and white Chinese screen that hides the radiator. If you can't see it, it's not there.

7:15 A.M.
I drag my bags back to the door. This time I remember my laptop. I check my purse for today's itinerary, scanning the crumpled and creased paper for the information I need. LaGuardia. American Airlines. Detroit. 9:00 A.M.

7:20 A.M.
"Apple Radio Cars, good morning."

"Good morning, I need a car . . ."

"I'm sorry. I can't hear you . . ."

"I need a car to LaGuardia."

"Where are you?"

"Nostrand between Clarkson and Lenox."

"Nostrandclarksonlenoxnostrandclarksonlenoxclarksonclarkson #89. Five minutes."

"What—I'm sorry."

"Five minutes. Your car will be there in five minutes."

"Oh, okay. Thank—"

click

7:25 A.M.

They say five, but they always mean ten. I need to change. The sweat-pants stay on, that way I won't lose them again. I put on my extra-large Oklahoma State sweatshirt. The hoodie envelops me in black fleece and covers my face. I feel hidden in it. Safe. Protected.

7:30 A.M.

I hear a honk outside. It's the car. I open the window and call out, "I'll be right there."

7:40 A.M.

I drag the bags down the stairs—open the door, and squint into the morning. I pull my bags behind me and the driver rushes out of his seat. He is not Hasaan. I watch, dazed, as he lifts the bags into the trunk. The sidewalk is dotted with people. Children in their school uni-forms still wiping the sleep from their eyes, the old women and their plastic bags shuffling to the train station, women my age, dressed in crisp suits, their hair shiny and perfect. I look after them longingly and then down at my faded sweatpants and stained, oversized sweatshirt.

I wonder what I'm doing wrong.

7:42 A.M.

"You ready?" the driver asks, as he closes the trunk.

"Just one second," I say, "I need to run to the bodega."

"Okay, miss." He opens the driver's side and eases into the front seat.

7:45 A.M.

"Mamita!" The bodega owner greets me as I enter the store. "Where you been?"

"Hi." I manage a smile. "I had to go away for—for work."

"They work you too hard?" He laughs.

I laugh with him, pretend it's not true. Notice instead his English is improving.

"Your English is so good."

"Yeah, my son." He smiles. "He say I'm fast learner. What you need, mami?"

"Red Bull."

He points to the back and says, "You know."

I walk to the cooler, stand there trying to figure out how many energy drinks it will take to propel me towards the day. I try to remember how many it took yesterday. Four. I open the door and pull out six and a bottle of Vitaminwater Focus. I juggle the cans and bottle and dump them on the counter.

"Anything else, mami?" I shake my head.

"Okay. For you? $6.50. You want bagel?"

"Are you sure?" I wonder how he makes money with all the breaks he gives me. I hand him a $10 bill and tell him to keep the change. "I have a car outside waiting."

"Take the bagel." He looks concerned, so I accept it.

"Gracias."

He laughs at my awkward pronunciation.

"At least you try. Have a good day, mami. Eat the bagel."

I thank him again, this time in English.

7:50 A.M.
Outside, the driver has his black Lincoln already running. I open the door and settle into the vinyl backseat.

"LaGuardia. American Airlines."

He tunes the radio and settles on a station. Creole flows from the speakers. *He's Haitian. You should ask his name.*

I don't care, I say to myself.

"You say something?" the driver asks, turning slightly.

"Do you want a bagel?"

"No, thank you."

The car pulls away from the curb and I take one last look at my neighborhood, then I look away and pull the first Red Bull out of the bag. I crack it open and hear the familiar hiss and bubble of the liquid inside. I press the can to my lips and drink.

7:55 A.M.
"So where are you off to?"

"Detroit."

I finish the first can and reach for the second. In just a few minutes the caffeine will flood my veins.

8:00 A.M.
He nods and says nothing else. I hesitate before I reach for a third can and decide against it. I'll need something for the plane. I sigh loudly and lean back, but I don't close my eyes, only stare up at the cracked and peeling ceiling of the car. I reach up and pull a loose, hanging thread. It unravels the stitching and bits of it flake and fall onto the seat. I know the driver is watching me in the rearview mirror. I put my hand back in my lap, feeling guilty.

"So how long have you been driving?"

The driver's grin is wide and friendly. He sits up in his seat. "This is my second week." I ask him how he likes it as the car speeds along the Jackie Robinson Parkway. I ask him another question and stare out of the window as the driver's chatter rises and falls around me. I pull out another Red Bull and pepper his rapid, gilded speech with well-placed, "*um hmmms*" and "*really*s."

8:20 A.M.
My heart and stomach drop and swirl as the airport draws near. I immediately reach for the fourth can of Red Bull.

8:25 A.M.
The driver leaps from the car to help me with my luggage. I hand him more money than I should. He smiles and wishes me a safe trip. I nod, grab my things in both hands, and head towards the doors.

8:30 A.M.
It's not so much the traveling.

What It Feels Like

REMEMBER THE FIRST TIME you were ever on a Ferris wheel? Remember when you got to the very top and just sat there, the entire world at your feet? You could see everything. You felt like you could reach up and grab the sky. Your entire body tingled with this intersection of joy and indestructibility and fearlessness and that good anxious recklessness. So fucking excited to be alive at that moment. You could do anything.

Now imagine feeling that every day for a week, or a month, or a few months. Twenty-four hours a day, seven days a week, without a break. No "down." No rest. So that everything you do feels like THE BIGGEST MOST AMAZING THING YOU HAVE EVER DONE IN YOUR LIFE!

The first week or so, it's great. You write and memorize dozens of new poems. You reach out to old friends you've lost touch with. You make new friends on the subway platform and on the third floor of Barnes & Noble and in line at Jamba Juice. You spend hours on the steps of Union Square Park watching the skateboarders and NYU students, imagining what their lives must be like. And these are all beautiful things because everything is beautiful.

Everything is beautiful.

Until it's not.

Because then the insomnia sets in. And you're stacking days on top of each other, adding a new one before the last one ends. And you find yourself unable to settle down and focus on anything for long. You *have* to write the entire book tonight before you can sleep or eat or leave the house or do anything. But first you *have* to call your friends and your sister and the guy you just met and tell them all how much you love them. Tell each one that you've never felt this way about any other human being in the entire world and you're so lucky and so glad and so grateful to have such an amazing, magical person in your life. And you believe it because it's true.

Until it isn't. Until everything about them—the way their voices trail, the way their mouths move when they chew, the fact that he crosses his legs at the knee, the way she speaks about movies she's never seen, the way they refer to celebrities by their first names—starts to make you feel like your blood is filled with snakes and you want to scream awful things at them about how the sounds of their voices feel like teeth on your skin and how much you hate their mother or their apartment or yourself. You want to bury your hatred in them but you're never quite sure who you hate the most. You, it's always you. And you're afraid they will see how ugly and damaged you are, or how much you wish your heart would slow down so that you could forget you're alive, but you need them to remind you that you're alive so you beg the men to love you, because to convince them that you are worth it means you can one day convince yourself. So you invite them to live in your mouth and in your body until they tire of you, which you know will happen because you have tired of you. And you want to beg the friends to see you—past the smile and the jokes—to see that you are a dying and bloody being standing empty in front of them.

You know how you can get a song stuck in your head? Imagine hearing that song even in your sleep—waking you up in the middle of the night to ensure you're aware of the lap it's running in your head. Then imagine you *have* to find out everything you can about that song and its singer. Where it started. Who wrote it. What inspired it. Why. You have to do all of this before there can be quiet in your head, before you can rest, before you can sleep.

Now, imagine you do this with people. Someone you just met or someone you've known for a while but barely thought of until that random day when you bumped into him and now you *have* to see him all the time and call and text and be available when he wants to hang out and feel like you've been thrown away any time you can't reach him for any reason.

Now imagine all this with shoes and with clothes and with food. You *have* to have a grande chai with almond milk and three stevia, or a veggie burrito bowl but only from Chipotle, or a waffle at every restaurant in Manhattan that sells them. Your day will make no sense unless you have that burrito bowl, or those waffles, or that Orange Dream Machine smoothie from Jamba Juice.

Until one day the thought of food makes you sick. The plate is too big, and the food drips and runs into itself till you see nothing but a congealed mass of fat that you imagine attached to your hips and rounding your thighs. You become a vegan. You decide you can no longer stomach anything white or red or pink. Then you can only eat green and yellow food until even that is too much, so water. Only water. And Red Bull because it's clear.

And clothes—the designer that makes the only clothes that fit you, that you're comfortable in. Everything else is too heavy, too rough against your skin, doesn't fit the curves you still pretend to have. You can only wear 7 For All Mankind jeans or Citizens of Humanity because they were both created by the same people until one of them left because they had a falling out and started COH. You know this because you researched and Googled and Wiki-ed everything there is to know about them and those are the only jeans you can wear now so who cares if they're two hundred dollars? And then Oprah gave her entire audience James Perse T-shirts. She said they were the softest things she'd ever felt on her body and it's Oprah so you have to have them too. You have to have the T-shirt, and the long-sleeved T-shirt, and the Henley, and the off-the-shoulder in pink and white because you have suddenly discovered that you love your neck and shoulders. So you stay up all night and you order these shirts because Oprah said they were the softest she'd ever felt and you want to feel them. You want to know what they feel like and online shopping is the worst thing and the best thing that has ever happened to you because if you can't sleep because you can't stop thinking of the perfect jeans or the shirts so soft they made Oprah moan then you can just buy them and try them for yourself. And the Internet is the worst and the best thing that could have ever happened to you because you can always find out more information and feed your hungry brain and sometimes this will settle you down. Sometimes you know you have reached the end of this wire you've been balancing on but that same live wire reminds you that you need to keep moving and going and moving and going and social media is the worst and the best thing to happen to you because someone else is always awake too. Someone in Japan or Nigeria or London or Calabasas, and you can always find someone who will talk to you on ISCA or IRC and then later Friendster and MySpace and then Twitter and Facebook. Someone who will appreciate how you are always awake, someone who will appreciate how fast you type. You can't even write things down on paper anymore because your brain moves faster than your hand and even when you're careful your handwriting turns into illegible scrawls because your hand can't possibly keep up with your brain but thanks to chat rooms in college you can type almost as fast as your brain. Almost.

Now imagine you do this with people you know. Imagine you call and text and call and text and email and if you don't hear back you call and text and email again to make sure that you haven't offended them, that you haven't hurt them, then you call and text and call and text to apologize for calling and texting so much and then you send a follow-up email so they know how sorry you are for whatever you did and also how pissed off you are that they won't even talk to you about it because how were you supposed to know you did this terrible thing if they didn't even tell you about it and you decide that you don't need friends like that in your life so you block them and delete them and decide fuck them, you don't need them. You don't need them but then you're sorry for jumping to conclusions and being upset before you hear them out because what if you did do something awful but forgot and they have been trying to reach you but you blocked them so you unblock only you can't remember the numbers and you deleted them to keep yourself from calling and now you want to tell them that you're sorry, that you didn't mean to block or delete them, and now you can't and everything is ruined and now you have to stop being friends with them because you are poison. You are not a good person and now you're crying because you've ruined your friendship, or you spent the rent money and the bill money on Oprah's favorite things or on eBay and your roommate will find out when the electricity is cut off. (But it's all okay actually because you never buy big-ticket items. You never put down a thousand dollars on a pair of shoes or a hat or a bag. Your purchases make sense. They are justifiable. Though, the makeup was from MAC and not the drugstore. It lasted longer, was higher quality. Designer jeans, but from 7 For All Mankind, not Guess?—and they will last forever. You buy things that you use, that you need. And you buy things for other people. You are magnanimous. You buy things for your parents and your siblings and your friends and you pick up the checks at restaurants. Houses and cars could be repossessed but they can't take your jeans or your dresses or your shoes or the money you spent on friends and family. They can't take you. They couldn't fit all of your body and all the sleepless and restless nights into normal. They couldn't take you.)

Now imagine you can't sleep because you have this song stuck in your head because you saw this actor in Union Square Park and realized he lives in your neighborhood and you imagined what it would be like to be his friend and so you found every single episode of this show he was in that you just read about and you have to watch it all from the very beginning tonight. You *have* to watch each and every episode. Tonight. And you *have* to sing that song. And that's what you're doing instead of being normal. Instead of sleeping. And that actor. You wonder what it would be like to be friends with him. And you wonder what it would be like to be someone who sleeps. And you think that if you were friends with this actor then you would be okay. You have to work at being normal and regular and human and normal but he would be able to help. He would encourage you to sleep, say things like "You still up? Girl, go to bed." And you'd laugh because that's so you. So you to not sleep. So you to be awake and worrying. And you don't need those friends that don't call back and the boys who won't write back because now you're gonna be friends with him. Now you just gotta find him. But first you gotta sleep.

Or listen to that song again. Or send that email. Or watch that movie.

And imagine you do all of this each night for many nights in a row and in those rare moments when you can settle your brain down enough to close your eyes you sleep like a fugitive. As though every sound and movement is entering your body and waking you, as though every sound and movement exists to keep you awake and alert in case you have to run or fight or remind yourself that you're still alive. And you are and you're relieved but now you're also awake again and the fatigue has entered your blood. And then the packages come because of course you did overnight express and the phone calls get returned and the texts and emails answered and you feel crazy and stupid and silly and irresponsible and you're exhausted because you know this isn't normal. You know this isn't how normal people are and you don't know what's wrong with you. And you don't know what to do. And you don't know how to live like this but you don't know how to stop and the need to convince your body to give up is visceral—it crawls through your being and your brain wants to stop it but your brain can't because your brain is tired.

Imagine you don't fit anywhere, not even in your own head.

Beauty in the Breakdown

ER FACE IS WET. These days, the tears appear so quietly she doesn't even notice the leak until her face is drenched. She's learned to be silent, to allow the tears to fall without a whimper or sob. She is waiting for the threat of water to leave before she moves.

She doesn't know how long she's been lying there. She remembers letting room service in after rehearsal. The attendant didn't bat an eye when she asked him to put the tray on the floor. The platter of fruit lies untouched alongside a pitcher of water, just a few inches from her head. The ice cubes have long melted and she stares at the pitcher, hypnotized by the condensation tracing a wild pattern down its sides. The sky outside the hotel window is black and starless. She knows it's almost time to leave, but dreads Chicago's January cold wrapping itself around her already shivering body.

She closes her eyes and feels the rough of the carpet against her cheek. Moves her face slowly back and forth until there's a slight burn. She wants to rub her face raw, scar her cheek, so that she's too disfigured to go onstage.

You have to get up.

Call time is 7:00. The clock reads 6:50.

Fuck. She has to get to the theater. The floor rushes up to meet her as she stands. She grabs her bag, too nice for the way she abuses it—the way she abuses anything beautiful. She stuffs her feet into a pair of slippers, then hesitates at the door, unsure why she finds it so difficult to leave today: this heaviness attached itself to her feet. She is usually able to hold herself together with promises of returning to her room, but not now. She scans the room one more time: the uniformly polite hotel decor at war with the upturned suitcases and disheveled, unmade beds. She hopes one of these things will somehow give her a reason to stay. She has none.

In the lobby of the hotel she sees her cast members leaving for the theater a few steps ahead of her. They often meet before and after shows to drink and party. She always rushes past them after curtain, stripping off her costume and pulling her hoodie tight around her face. Their eyes stab through the fleece covering her. She knows they whisper about her. About how weird she has become. How she never talks anymore. How it has all gone to her head, made her standoffish and arrogant.

Nobody ever asks her if something's wrong.

Outside the Chicago wind attacks her, a reminder that she's forgotten her coat and is wearing slippers during a Chi-Town winter. The cold takes hold of her bones and forces her to feel, so she welcomes it. Head down, she hurries to the theater, avoiding the strange looks from passersby, properly bundled against the cold.

When she enters the theater, she's overwhelmed once again by its grandness. The high, painted ceilings, the thousands of gold and velvet seats surrounding the stage. Soon this place will be filled. Soon she will have to pretend everything is okay and perform. She should have stayed in the hotel room. She should have called the stage manager and told her she wasn't feeling well.

Alice, the stage manager, has been with the show since Broadway and saw them through the month in Edinburgh on through the current US tour. Alice is beautiful—the color of stucco and sunshine, her hair a thick lion's mane of gray locs dancing down her back. Once, during a show in Atlanta, she called her in for a meeting. She remembers that Alice's hotel room smelled like spice and peace. She remembers staring at her smooth, lineless face, wondering if she herself would make it to sixty and, if she did, could she allow herself to possibly be so beautiful? She remembers wanting to reach out and touch Alice's face, as though if she touched something beautiful and worthy of life maybe it would enter her and she would be the same.

"Are you okay?" Alice had asked. Even her voice was a confection.

She immediately produced a PR smile, teeth exposed like she's close to a laugh, the one that never reaches her eyes.

No, said her brain.

"What do you mean?" said her wide mouth, the smile shifting slightly.

She could see Alice surveying the way her clothes hung on her. She didn't want any more questions, so before Alice could speak again, she said, "I had a bad breakup recently. I'm just still dealing with it."

She held a steady gaze with Alice's gray eyes as she lied. Broken hearts are easier to explain—how do you tell someone your brain is broken? So she babbled, a contrived story of hurt and betrayal, combined with the truths of the days awake, the hotel floors soaked with her salt. The story wound tightly around her tongue, even squeezing out a few more tears.

"So you see, it's just been difficult to adjust on the road," she finished, with her patented brave-but-sad small smile.

Alice nodded after the story ended, but she could tell the older woman didn't believe her. As she stood to leave, Alice held her by the shoulders, her hands heavy on the thin bones, and stared at her. The anxiety began to bubble in her chest and she knew it would grow if she didn't leave soon. She stared at Alice's face until it blurred and melted away, allowing whatever words Alice was offering to race out of the room ahead of her. When she turned to leave, Alice's voice hung sweet and spiced behind her: "It doesn't have to be like this."

For a moment, she stopped at the door, something urging her to tell Alice what little truth she knows of this thing. Her back to the room, the ball in her chest grew and grew. She had to leave, before it exploded into pieces she couldn't contain. She opened the door and walked out.

That was a month ago. Since then, she's grown quieter, thinner. She used to welcome Alice's presence, but she's had to close the door on her as well. Sitting in her dressing room, she tries to find herself in the reflection. She pulls faces, twisting her features into grotesque and contorted masks. She exhales, cheeks puffed. She's trying to remember what her normal face looks like. This face is too drawn, cheekbones so sharp they could cut cocaine. She's not sure that makeup can fix this, but she starts with the dark circles under her eyes. Her makeup bag holds the witchcraft that will hopefully make her look human again.

She dabs her face with the liquid foundation, smears the brown across her forehead, her nose, under her eyes, across her chin. War paint. She feels tears, rising from the back of her throat. She clears it and continues blending the streaks of foundation together. Her heart begins to race. She ignores it, pats setting powder on her face and neck. When her vision begins to blur, she closes her eyes and counts until it passes. She knows this place. Nerves about the show. No matter how many times she goes on stage, she still gets nervous. It's just anxiety. The sadness never follows her to the theater. Not once. Not once before. Not today. Curtain is at 8:00 and she still needs to get refitted for her costume.

She accelerates her makeup routine, rushing through eyelashes and eye shadow and eyeliner. She's on to lip liner when there's a knock on the door. She ignores it. She has to concentrate. The knock comes again, louder.

"It's Maxine. I have your stage clothes."

She throws a "Come in!" over her shoulder and gets back to her lips. Maxine, former Alvin Ailey dancer turned costumer, is tall and elegant—all fire and sass and Black Southern belle cliché. The first day they met, because she had joined the production so late, they spent hours scouring boutiques from Harlem to SoHo for stage and makeup looks. They had carried the bond from that day to the tour and become friends, but these days, they've become strangers again. She doesn't even look at Maxine when she enters.

Maxine quietly hangs the clothes on the rack. "Do you know which outfit you're wearing tonight?" she asks the reflection in the mirror.

"No. Anything but the jeans. I hate those tacky stretch things. I bought a pair of Citizens to replace them." She's tired of all this talking. "I gave them to your assistant before y'all left for New Zealand. He was supposed to hem them." She just wants to hurry through her makeup so she can make it through the show and back to the hotel.

"Why didn't you bring them directly to me?" Maxine asks.

"Does it really matter now? I need to finish." She doesn't know why she's being so rude, only that she needs to be angry at someone else. The anger she holds for herself is exhausting.

Curtain is at 8:00.

Maxine's face falls into confused concern. She opens her mouth to speak, then shuts it again and leaves without another word.

It's remarkable how quickly loneliness takes up space in the room.

The silence is broken by a PA announcement, "Thirty minutes till curtain!"

She inhales sharply, her heartbeat increasing again, and fixes her gaze on her reflection—an empty space, covered in makeup. Her eyelashes are crooked, but nobody will see that shit from the audience anyway. She needs to finish her mouth. She reaches in her makeup bag for a tube of Film Noir lipstick. She finds tubes of lip gloss. Eye shadows. Mascara. More makeup brushes. More lipsticks. No Film Noir. She dumps the contents of the bag on the table and begins to frantically search through them, items scattering and rolling onto the floor. She feels the quiver start at her bottom lip before radiating through her body like some evil superpower. She has to find Film Noir or everything will fall apart. She drops to her hands and knees, crawls to the gold Melie Bianco bag she tossed on the floor when she entered. She dumps the contents out too. *Don't cry. Don't cry. Don't cry. Don't cry.*

She searches through piles of nothing looking for her lipstick, until the panic hits her head and the room begins to sway. She can't breathe. Gasping, she continues to pillage, her fingers trembling. If she finds it, it will be okay. It will all stop. If she finds it, she will make it through the show and back to the hotel. If she finds it, there will be no tears tonight. If she finds it, there will be trays of food—something other than fruit.

She finds it. Lodged in a side pocket. There is no relief. The anxiety has already infiltrated.

"Call time in fifteen minutes, people!"

No. She needs more time. She needs to calm down. She jumps up and down and shakes her whole body, an old acting exercise. She needs this to stop. The first tear falls. She brushes it away and rushes to the mirror, pulling Kleenex from the vanity and dabbing at her face. You can only dab. If you rub, the eyes will get red and swollen, so she dabs and dabs and dabs but the tears come faster than she can dab them away, her face is still drenched and her body still forming small ripples. She has to reapply her makeup. She has fifteen minutes. She has to get dressed. Where is Maxine with her clothes? She has fifteen minutes to get her shit together. She has fifteen minutes until she has to smile and perform and laugh and act like a normal person for at least one hour of the day. She just needs to make it to intermission.

"Get your shit together," she tells her reflection. She dabs at her eyes again and an eyelash falls off, gliding to the floor like a butterfly wing. It lands just beneath the sink. She stares at it and then herself before getting on the floor to retrieve it.

There's a knock on the door. She finds she can't say anything.

She crawls under the sink, her body a tight ball, sobbing into her knees with the broken butterfly of an eyelash clutched in her fist.

Another knock. And then another. She buries her face in her knees and wills her body to shrink into nothing.

Outside she hears Maxine, irritated. "You need to get dressed! Curtain is in ten minutes!" The door opens sharply, Maxine in preshow panic. The other woman stops short when she sees her trembling and whimpering underneath the sink.

"Oh baby . . ." Maxine says, starting towards her.

"Go. Get. Alice. Please."

Maxine drops the clothes and rushes out of the room. She's back in seconds with Alice, who takes one look and crawls under the sink. Alice holds her, stroking her hair as years of rivers flood over.

"It's okay. I got you." Still honey and spice, Alice's voice sinks into her skin. "I got you, baby . . . I got you now but if you don't get help, you're going to die."

She closes her eyes and clings to Alice, the ball in her chest now a helpless pool of panic broken open, flooding her.

It Has a Name

FOLDED MYSELF INTO THE guest chair and stared through the woman sitting in front of me. This one, Dr. Tiago, was different. She had long brown hair that fell and skimmed her waist. I wondered if she brushed it every night. I wanted to ask her why she didn't put it in a ponytail or braid, why she just let it hang loose and straight down her back like that. Didn't the wind ever mess it up? Or did it just swing vaguely as she walked?

Right now, Dr. Tiago and her hair were staring at me, waiting for me to speak. Or maybe answer a question? I closed my eyes, trying to remember what it was that I was supposed to say. The other doctors, I saw today, were easier. I had wanted them to tell me that I was normal, so I'd told them things that made me seem normal. I had pasted a smile on my face, sat with my legs crossed, left foot swinging. I had lifted all the charm I had saved in that last still-capable part of my soul. I made sure they'd understood that it was all a misunderstanding. I was stressed. I was hungry. I was homesick. I was tired. None of them had noticed that I was sitting calmly in front of them, hands folded on my lap, plunging headfirst off a cliff. But by the time the wind had carried me into Dr. Tiago's office, I was bone-less. Bloodless. So I sat in this guest chair and stared through her.

I wondered what her background was. She looked Filipina but also white—except Tiago isn't a white person's name. I checked her fingers for rings and saw none. She looked like the kind who would wear a wedding or engagement or promise ring. She looked like the kind who liked being claimed. I'm sure someone had told her that he liked her hair, long and curtain-like. I wondered if she had many friends. She seemed studious but fun. Not a sorority girl type at all. I tried to imagine this gray pantsuit in front of me as an undergrad, clutching a red cup, drunken *Girls-Gone-Wild* scream into a camera. The image made the corners of my mouth twitch in and out of the beginnings of a smile.

"What are you smiling about?" Dr. Tiago's voice had the clipped precision of someone whose first language isn't English.

"Nothing. Just thought of something." I folded myself most tightly into the chair and dropped my head. *No more questions.*

"I want to ask you some questions, is that okay?"

"You can ask anything you want. What I answer is a different thing." I didn't mean for it to sound as abrasive as it felt leaving my tongue. I looked up to make sure she understood that.

Dr. Tiago smiled. "That's fine. These are just a series of questions that will help me determine how best to help you. Just answer: None of the time, some of the time, or all of the time. Do you ever have extreme mood changes from happy to sad? Or vice versa?"

"All of the time."

"Do you have trouble with sleep? Either oversleeping or not sleeping at all?"

"All of the time."

"Do you find it difficult to eat or find yourself binging on food?"

My stomach folded a bit, reminding me that if you stop eating long enough, the hunger disappears. "Some of the time to the first and none of the time to the second."

"Do you ever have thoughts of suicide or harming yourself?"

The air in the room stopped moving. I didn't say anything, afraid to disturb the quiet the question had created.

Dr. Tiago cocked her head, her eyes unreadable, and waited patiently for an answer. A few more seconds passed, the silence continuing to build between us. I pushed away the weeks and months and years that answered her question.

"No."

Dr. Tiago straightened up in her chair. "Is that an honest answer?"

"Yes."

"Then why the hesitation?"

"Because I've never wanted to kill myself. That's what that means, right? 'Thoughts of suicide or harming myself?' I haven't."

She leaned forward, her thick dark hair swishing to one side. "What have you thought of?"

I sat across from her, daring myself not to cry. Once it started, I wouldn't be able to keep myself together. I held the words on my tongue, rolling them around in my mouth prepared to spit them out, as bitter as they felt. "I don't want to die."

"That's not what I asked you."

For the first time, I matched her stare and repeated, "I don't want to die." I shifted my gaze to the window behind her. The tree outside appeared to lean toward me, waiting for me to finish.

"Opening my eyes every morning is a disappointment."

The doctor barely blinked at this revelation. She reacted to it as though it were normal. As if it was a thing people told her all the time. This was even less comforting than believing it was just me. Dr. Tiago put her intake papers to the side and leaned forward in her chair. I was starting to hate how her face held no expression.

"Are there times when you feel like you can do anything in the world? Like you're invincible?"

"Not lately."

"But you have before?"

"Sometimes."

"And then sometimes you feel like you can't do anything right? Is that what you feel now?"

The tears were at attention again. Soon, they would attack my face. I was too tired, too dry for a proper weeping so I waited for them to do as they pleased. One renegade tear fell down my face and then another but my body didn't have energy for any more after that.

Dr. Tiago stood and I was both afraid that she might hug me and hopeful that she would. Instead, she headed to her desk and sat on the corner near the phone. The abrupt nature of this shift in energy made me uncomfortable. So I sat up too, folded my hands on my lap, and recalled the face I'd offered the other doctors. I hoped that the session was over. I was frightened that the session was over. And still nothing from Dr. Tiago. No diagnosis. No words of comfort. Just her on the desk and me, without the bones to stay upright, I slumped again in yet another doctor's chair, eyes blank, concentrating on matching her for expressionlessness.

"Based on what we spoke about and your answers to the few questions I asked you"—she was halfway through the sentence before I realized she was speaking—"I want to refer you to my colleague, Dr. Goodman. He's a psychiatrist and he may be able to help further." As her words made their way towards me, the fatigue ruling my body turned her face into a shapeless mess of features.

"What's wrong with me?" My heart quickened its march in my chest as I thought of all the possibilities. Just one really: *I'm crazy.* I already knew that though. The question was how crazy. "I'm not going to a hospital."

"No. I don't think you need a hospital but you do need some more evaluation that I'm not qualified to give. I have my suspicions but Dr. Goodman will give you a proper diagnosis. He's on Fifty-Sixth and Eighth. Let me call him and see if he can see you immediately."

"That's okay. I don't need. I don't need any more doctors . . ." My voice broke and those goddamn tears finally found the courage to stream down my face though my body was still too tired for the sobbing that they demanded. I couldn't steady my brain enough to leave.

Dr. Tiago handed me a box of tissues and a look of—pity? Empathy? Irritation? I took a few begrudgingly.

"Can he tell me how to get my life back?"

Dr. Tiago picked up the phone and had a hushed conversation with this "Dr. Goodman." She hung up and turned to me. "He says he can see you now. You just need to get to his office."

"What's wrong with me?"

For the first time, Dr. Tiago's face softened, her hair even seemed to relax a bit. "There's nothing 'wrong' with you, but there may be something that needs to be treated. Dr. Goodman will explain."

"I'm not going to a hospital," I repeated.

"No hospital. I promise." Dr. Tiago grabbed a slip of paper from her organized desk. I imagined her apartment was just as tidy. Nothing moved out of its place. Not even her hair. Dr. Tiago handed me the slip of paper with a number and address on it.

"He's expecting you."

She stood, walked to the door, and opened it. I'd been dismissed. I made my way to leave, clutching the paper in my hand. I was seconds away from balling it up. As if reading my mind, Dr. Tiago said again, with added sternness in her tone, "He's expecting you."

I can't remember if I said thank you or even goodbye. I just remember standing in front of Dr. Tiago's building, the chill of New York winter attacking me. I looked down at the now-wrinkled paper in my hand. I recognized the address. It was near Barneys. Barneys, where I had blown many a paycheck. The shoe floor alone was a second home. I remember I wondered if maybe I should just go there instead.

⋕

DR. GOODMAN'S OFFICE WAS in a posh, doormanned building on the East Side. An older woman in a fur coat so big she looked like a yeti was making her way out. I stared a bit too long when I noticed one of her sleeves had dark eyes staring back at me—a dog so small, it looked battery operated. She surveyed my own outfit as she passed, determining if I was someone who deserved a doormanned building and proximity to obnoxious fur coats. I looked down at the jeans hanging off my hips like a mistake. My black suede Pumas suddenly felt more Brooklyn than Upper West Side. I crossed my arms to shield myself from her judgment, suddenly feeling too poor and too Black to even be in her presence. Never mind that everything I wore was designer. My out-of-control shopping habit had high-end tastes but to the average observer, I looked sick. Too thin. Hollowed, blank eyes. Sunken face. It didn't matter if I was wearing Prada or Payless.

The elevator to the eleventh floor was mirrored and slow. I couldn't escape the refracted images of myself so I stared at my shoes, feeling my toes pressed against the leather. I had forgotten to put on socks. Or a coat. It was January.

The elevator ding brought me back to where I was and why. I was grateful to have the waiting room to myself. I took the seat furthest from the door. I needed the window to remind me that the outside world still existed. I grabbed a *People* magazine from the coffee table in front of me and thumbed through it before deciding that *Time* would probably make a better first impression. Maybe the magazines were a test. *Time* would definitely make me look more serious. Less crazy. If that was still possible. I stared at the magazine, trying to care about the recent science something of the biological something else. I couldn't, but before I could toss *Time* and pick up *People* again, a small pale man appeared at the waiting room entrance. He smiled at me and said, "I'm Dr. Goodman. You must be my three o'clock."

I always loved how doctors did that, referred to you as the time of your appointment. My memory was a patchwork, and names and faces often fell through the holes in the stitching. I wished I could adopt a similar reference system: "Hi, you must be my four P.M. conversation from last week." I almost laughed to myself then remembered where I was. I needed to keep the self-talk at bay. I followed Dr. Goodman down a dark hall out of sync with the posh, doormanned building. The space in his office was cramped, every wall and bookshelf stuffed with hundreds—no, thousands—of books. There were more piled in various places in the room. Some looked dangerously close to toppling over.

"Have you read all these books?"

"Most of them," he answered. "All of them actually. But over decades."

"Wow." I glanced around the room trying to pick out a book I recognized. Most were psychology texts and papers with plastic covers, but I spotted *The Iliad* and Dante's *Inferno*.

Dr. Goodman pointed me to a leather couch near the window. I kept forgetting what I was here for.

"So," he began. "Dr. Tiago said that you've been having some difficulties."

"Some difficulties." I liked that better than "going crazy." "Difficulties" sounded like all I needed was tutoring or extra credit to pass the normal test.

"Can you tell me a little bit about what's been happening recently?"

I was tired of this story already. I had told it so often today. Sometimes I exaggerated one aspect over the other.

"He's expecting you." Dr. Tiago's voice urged me towards truth. I closed my eyes as tight as I could, took a breath, and fired my story at him. College. Elementary school. That one time when I was eight and third grade was hard. Back to college. My first time in New York. Freshman year of college. The tour. The whirlwind in my head had shown up again after being blissfully mute all day. The words seemed to throw themselves off my tongue, my brain struggling to order and control them. I wasn't sure if I was making sense or even answering the question at all. I stopped midsentence.

I couldn't look at Dr. Goodman. I stared at my hands, folded in my lap, left foot crossed over my right knee and swinging. The silence in the room felt like another person. Dr. Goodman stood up and went to a desk, significantly less tidy than Dr. Tiago's. He rooted through the papers on it until he produced a folder. He pulled out a form, attached it to a clipboard with a pen chained to it, and handed it to me.

"I need you to fill this out to the best of your ability."

I looked up at him, past his face, past the wall of books, past the dingy hallway, past the doorman, and imagined myself outside. Free from these questions.

"They are a more detailed list of questions than the ones Dr. Tiago asked you. Just answer the best you can." His voice held New York dearly. I wanted to hear him say "cawfee" and "tawk." I wanted him to tell me about his life. I wanted to ask about his family and his books and the stack of magazines and the woman with the fur coat and the dog. I didn't want to do this.

"He's expecting you," Dr. Tiago and her curtain of hair reminded me.

I looked down at the form. And methodically answered: all of the time, some of the time, none of the time, some of the time, all of the time, all of the time, all of the time, all of the time, none of the time, some of the time . . .

When I finished, I looked it over, taking more care than I ever had with the SATs. I handed the clipboard back to the doctor. He went over it silently and I studied him, trying to figure out what he was looking for—or, worse, what he was seeing. I could feel the thing begin to rise from my belly, and the light coating of perspiration that usually signaled the start of it.

Dr. Goodman leaned forward, still studying the form, his elbows resting on his brown over-creased slacks. I stared at his curly hair in need of a haircut. He looked like the kind of person that was always running a few minutes late. His tie hung around his neck like the last decision of the day. There was a faint stain on the pocket of his shirt.

"Cawfee" I bet.

I focused on the stripes of his shirt, counting the lines on his left arm. I had made it to thirty when he spoke.

"Based on everything you've told me," he began, "and your answers to the questionnaire—" *You're crazy.* My brain finished the sentence for him: "—my official diagnosis is mixed episode rapid cycling bipolar two disorder."

I didn't understand what any of those words meant together. The only one I recognized in context was not one I wanted.

"I'm not bipolar."

I thought of all the news stories I'd seen of violent, crazy, "bipolar people." They were always enraged and ran down the street naked and confused. I was far from violent and didn't even like to be naked in the shower. There had to be some mistake.

"I'm not bipolar," I repeated.

"Bipolar exists on a spectrum. Bipolar I is more extreme. It used to be called manic depression. You have bipolar II, which is characterized by bouts of depression and something called hypomania, which isn't as extreme as mania in bipolar one but does have its own set of worries. Things like irritability, decreased need for sleep while still high energy, reckless and impulsive behavior, sexual promiscuity, overspending of money, appearing larger than life, life of the party, inability to focus . . ."

My mind began to shut down as he continued to list what I knew as my personality. Hypomania. Compulsive. Fixation. Rapid speech. Hypersexual.

I needed him to stop talking. I needed him to stop using words that didn't apply to me. I needed him to say "crazy" or "not crazy." Instead, he was speaking to me in Doctor and my brain began its race again. And he was still talking—

"Most people with this disorder can go years between hypomania and depression. But rapid cyclers can go between hypomania and depression in a matter of days, sometimes even hours. They can start off the day manic and end it depressed." I didn't say anything—I knew it too well. "And mixed-episode means that sometimes you can experience hypomania and depression at the same time. That sounds like what you were experiencing on the tour. Unable to sleep or eat, but heavily depressed at the same time. Bipolar two is one of the easier treatable illnesses."

How do I exist as a crazy person? is what I really wanted to know.

"We can find medication for you. An antidepressant and then a mood stabilizer as well as an antianxiety med. We probably also need to put you on sleep meds until we can regulate your insomnia. There are plenty to choose from now. It's just about finding the right fit. Trial and error."

"How long before I'm cured?"

Dr. Goodman hesitated, pity visiting then leaving his face. "There is no cure."

The panic hit my chest first, then dropped into my belly. Soon the trembling would begin.

There has to be a cure. It's not AIDS or cancer, it's my stupid brain. It's stress. I need to sleep. I just need to remember what normal feels like so I can imitate it. I can pretend. I just need to remember. It can be cured. How long will it take? A month. Six months? A year? I will take a hundred pills until I'm cured. There has to be a cure.

But this thing had a name. Bipolar II. I had never heard of it. Never heard of any Black people with it, so unless I was the first there had to be some mistake.

"You will probably be on medication for the rest of your life." The words echoed and ricocheted off his books and landed at my feet. I tried to catch them as they fell but the spilling over was too quick. Dr. Goodman shuffled in his seat and gestured to a box of tissues next to me.

"I need to take it again." My voice sounded like it was coming from someone else. Somewhere else.

"I beg your pardon?"

"The questionnaire—" someone, somewhere said, "I need to take it again. I must have answered it wrong. Please let me take it again." My voice broke as anxiety attacked every word, so that I sounded the exact level of crazy I would have done anything to avoid.

Side Effects May Include

SIDE EFFECTS MAY INCLUDE: A SENSE OF BEING DETACHED FROM YOURSELF AND YOUR EMOTIONS. NERVOUSNESS, AGITATION, OR RESTLESSNESS.

SHE LAY IN HER bed staring at the ceiling trying to ignore the way every cell in her body seemed to crawl and slither under her skin.

What about under the kitchen sink?

It was 3:00 A.M. She had spent 9:00 P.M. on her hands and knees, toothbrush in hand scrubbing at the dust and dirt that lived under the radiator in the living room. She had spent 10:00 P.M. with a broom and mop, back and forth and back and forth, until the floor shined a distorted reflection back to her face.

But what about the kitchen sink?

The voice in her head had been pulsating and growing louder for the last four hours. She had organized the hall closet, making sure the Christmas lights were in a tidy bundle, the coats and jackets hung up according to color and thickness. Her jeans were all folded carefully and stacked three by three in her dresser.

What about the kitchen sink?

This was the fourth medication they had tried and she would have to call Dr. Goodman again—tell him that this one might have been working but had transformed her natural slovenliness into an uncomfortable orderliness. She could hear the air moving in her lungs every time she exhaled, the blood rushing through her veins, could feel her heart contract and expand with every beat. She buried her face in a pillow trying to stop the pull from bed to kitchen.

What about the kitchen sink? If you check under the sink and the sponges are in order, then we will rest, then we will sleep.

SIDE EFFECTS MAY INCLUDE: IMPAIRED COORDINATION. TREMBLING. FEELINGS OF DETACHMENT. IRREGULAR JERKY MOVEMENTS.

It made her shake so violently that climbing stairs was a slow, uncomfortable ordeal, holding a glass meant the contents would absolutely spill over.

"It's okay," her friends reassured her.

"It's okay," her family said, when her trembling hands sent a bowl of gravy onto the floor. They looked at her and each other as she burst into tears.

She placed a Thanksgiving call. "Dr. Goodman, I can't take this one either."

SIDE EFFECTS MAY INCLUDE: SLIGHT TREMORS. REPETITIVE SPEECH PATTERNS. DECREASED SEX DRIVE.

She invited an on-again and off-again friend-with-benefits to help with the loneliness none of the medications could cure. A photographer she'd met on a shoot years ago. She could feel herself vibrating on the couch next to him, vibrating underneath him as he kissed her on the couch, vibrating when she touched him.

"What's going on?" he asked as she pushed him away.

"I'm sorry I called you. I don't want to do this. I feel too . . . different . . ." Her voice trailed. "I feel too different," she repeated. "I feel too different," she said again. "I feel too different." Her brain was a skipping record. "I feel too different." Levi shook his head in confusion but she couldn't stop saying it. "I feel too different." She squeezed her eyes shut and compulsively beat her clenched fists against her lap. "I feel too different."

Levi grabbed her hands, trying to stop her from pounding bruises onto her thighs. "It's okay."

"I feel too different."

Later, as Levi slept—too polite to leave her alone—she huddled in the bathroom, whispering into the phone, "Dr. Goodman . . . I feel too different."

SIDE EFFECTS MAY INCLUDE: PARANOIA.

In his office, Dr. Goodman asked, "Has the depression improved?"

I nodded. After a few weeks, one day, it had felt like someone turned up a dimmer switch and everything around me seemed brighter—I didn't feel like crying as much anymore. So, yeah.

"I don't want to take you off that if it's working, but we need a stabilizer. You're cycling pretty quickly through the mixed-episodes: the hypomania and depression are concurrent and I'm concerned."

Me too.

"Let's try Geodon," Dr. Goodman said.

"I thought you said it was too expensive?"

"It is, but we've exhausted all the other options."

"I don't want to be numb or out of it. I still want to be able to feel."

Dr. Goodman sighed. We'd been through this before. The list of things I was concerned about was getting longer and longer: weight gain, weight loss, numbness, tremors, nausea.

"Let's just see how it goes," he told me. I could feel the irritation in his voice. I couldn't tell if my paranoia was warranted or yet another side effect, so I stopped resisting . . .

"Okay."

SIDE EFFECTS MAY INCLUDE: DROWSINESS. CONFUSION. GROG-
GINESS. EMOTIONAL DETACHMENT. ANTEROGRADE AMNESIA.

The first night, she drifted off to sleep with a smile. *It's working . . .
this one is working . . .* she made a mental note to tell Dr. Goodman. She had barely finished the thought before she was fast asleep.
When she woke, she was disappointed to see darkness outside her
window. She had gone to bed at 10:00 P.M. and couldn't believe
she'd only slept a couple of hours.

Her eyelids felt thick and heavy like drapery. She felt shackled to the bed.
Her body was out of sync with her mind, her movements delayed, like
a slow-motion replay. She decided to look at the clock. It felt as though
five minutes passed before her head finally turned in its direction. The
clock said 6:00 P.M. *I must have set it wrong,* she thought. Or there had
been an outage overnight. Or it meant 6:00 A.M. But her phone con-
firmed that it was, in fact, 6:00 P.M.; she had been asleep for twenty hours.

"Hello, Dr. Goodman . . ." She slurred into the phone.

"We'll cut the dosage."

She wanted something to work. She was tired of being someone who
couldn't be fixed by medicine. She just wanted to find the cure so she
could return to her old life. She tried the new dosage. She made sure
to check that the clock on her nightstand was synced with her cell
phone and her watch and the ticking clock in the living room. She
didn't want to be confused again when she woke up.

✳

HER BRAIN WOKE UP first and it took a series of commands for her
eyes to get the message *Wake up, Bass. Wake up.* She checked the

clock. This time, she had slept for sixteen hours. She supposed that was better but her body still felt like it was swimming in cold oatmeal. She could barely keep her slow eyes open. Every blink was an invitation to fall back asleep. She found herself nodding off.

Her head snapped back up, remembering a scene from the movie, *Lady Sings the Blues*—Diana Ross as Billie Holiday on stage in front of a microphone, the heroin making its way through her body. She stands, her eyes half open, her words slurred, nodding and snapping her head back up whenever she drifts. That scene took her to another: Diana Ross as Billie Holiday locked in an insane asylum. Pawing at the walls, wild and crazed, caged.

That's your future, her brain told her. *Is that what you want?*

"No," she said, the word oozing like slime out of her mouth and crawling down her chin. "No."

Life Sentence

IT HAD BEEN TEN months since Dr. Goodman had said, "You will probably be on meds for the rest of your life." To him, I'm sure it was just a perfunctory part of his job. He rattled it off, "You will probably need to be on medication for the rest of your life," as casually as reminding his wife to pick up milk that evening, "You'll probably need to get milk . . ."

For the rest of your life.

I was sure he'd already forgotten the words before he'd said them, but I'd been holding on to them like prophecy ever since. *The rest of your life. The rest of your life. The rest of your life. The rest of your life. The rest of your life.*

The part of it that gripped me the most depended on which side of my brain I was living in at that moment. When I was struggling with the hypomania it was *need medication*. . . . When I was in the darker, colder part of my brain, *for the rest of your life* felt like a sentence to life without parole. An eternity of feeding myself pills morning and night, attempting to manage a brain forever splitting and reconnecting at will. I didn't want that.

What I wanted, was a quick fix. I wanted the diagnosis to serve as a way of rebuilding my old life—one featuring a Bassey who was, if not fully "normal," a hell of a lot closer to it. I'd imagined bipolar medication would work like antibiotics. I would take it for a few months and clear up the infection and then go on with my life. *For the rest of your life* was a legal disclaimer. It was for the people who wouldn't try as hard as I would to be well. All I had to do was try and it would only be a matter of time before I joined the "normal."

I would be one of those people who woke up and ate breakfast and showered and brushed my teeth and got dressed and put on makeup and went somewhere because I had somewhere to go and people who expected me there. I would sit with them at lunch or in a meeting, emulating their "normal." The way she swung her leg, one shoe dangling from her toes. The way he tapped his glass when he was deep in thought. The way that one nodded and murmured along, able to easily focus and pay attention without a brain that always wandered off. Movements so beautiful that they appeared choreographed, even as they were the picture of nonchalance. Normal people without legs or hands that shook violently. Without anxiety constantly gripping them, or words shooting from their mouths before their brains could connect to approve them. People who weren't impulsive, or out of control. With movements that were purposeful. Direct. Whose days weren't ordered by a series of pills and doctors' instructions. People who walked around with full brains and no medications—*for the rest of your life*—I wanted to be like them desperately.

But every time I quit the meds, this thing returned and it was never the half-welcomed mania that awaited me, it was always the cavern.

Always the place where my brain told me that I was worthless and the world was better off without me. Always a pain so deep that it seemed to go through my body, ricochet off the walls, and land back in my stomach again. A pain so deep it's hard to explain and when you do it sounds dramatic but it's the only way to get close to the truth. As though someone had taken a hammer to my soul and smashed it over and over, then forced me to walk barefooted on these broken shards of myself. A soul pain. It was nameless and persistent, and I hated it more than anything in the world because it meant I was broken. It meant I was unfixable. It meant that I would never be free of the pills lined up on my dresser like soldiers ready for a war I didn't want to fight. I was tired of fighting.

"It's all about balance," Dr. Goodman had told me.

But really it was all about bartering, attempting to figure out what side effects I could live with—the ones that didn't make me gain weight and didn't make me lose weight and didn't make me drowsy and didn't make me nervous and didn't make me stupid. We had gone through the ones that made me vomit, the ones that made me feel nothing, the ones that made me feel too much, the ones that made me forget things seconds after I did them, and the one that made it difficult for me to speak, the words catching in my throat like a bullet in a jammed gun.

I stood in my bedroom, the bottles staring arrogantly back at me, waiting for me to pick them up, tip their pills into my hand, and swallow them *for the rest of your life.*

#

IT HAD STARTED WHEN Mr. Lathan had called to "let me go." I was fired; wouldn't be asked back to the tour. I didn't know what I was supposed to do for work or for money or with my days. They said it was for my own health. They said it was so I could take care of myself without the stress and pressures of the tour. They said I was an insurance risk. That they couldn't afford to have me break and crumble. They needed someone they could count on to hold themselves together. They wanted someone who didn't need pills to keep them stable. They didn't want me. I had treated the medications like an offering, begging the universe to grant me my life back. But after all of this I still couldn't reclaim what I'd lost. So what was the point?

For the rest of your life. It echoed inside me as I stared at the bottles on my dresser.

There wasn't a point and I wasn't going to do it anymore. I would just work harder at saving myself. No more pills required.

I wanted to make a production of it—find a beach and a breeze to see how hard I could throw the bottles, how far the wind would take them. I picked one up and went outside, to find a breeze, avoiding the eyes of the people walking up and down Nostrand Avenue as I hurried to the alley next to the bodega. It was still early evening so there were more folks out than usual. The sidewalks were filled with all these people who knew where to go: hurrying to get home and make dinner or rest after a long day, young girls holding each other and laughing as they walked. For a moment, I forgot my purpose in front of the building. What was my purpose? To be normal. To be like one of those women or laughing children. To be like my sister, so settled and focused, or my friends who sat in offices five days a week, or Tosin, married and building a life and a future with her new husband. They were normal; these pills were preventing me from being like them. I wanted to be someone whose brain knew how to work. I didn't want the extra help, especially "help" that brought its own set of problems. The pills were keeping me from my life.

I would stop drinking after tonight. I would stop eating sugar. I would Google natural ways to cure depression and I would do all of them. I would handle stress like everybody else. I would try yoga again! No. Yoga was still terrible, like a game of Simon Says with no winner. But I would stop eating or drinking or doing anything in order to keep this thing away for the rest of my life without the pills. I imagined throwing my arm back like a quarterback and tossing the bottle as far as I could. I imagined watching it sail through the air and bounce against the building and the open, overflowing Dumpster and, then, I imagined them rolling back and landing again at my feet. No, I needed to guarantee that they would be gone forever.

I went back into the apartment and into the bathroom, collected the remaining bottles from the bedroom on my way. I stood in front of the toilet staring at the artificial blue of the toilet bowl cleanser. It looked like a child's painting of the ocean. I thought about the breeze the last time I was near a beach. Miami performing at the Soul Beach Music Festival. I closed my eyes and tried to remember the breeze coming off the balcony of my hotel room that day.

I opened my eyes and peered down again, still clutching the pill bottles. The toilet looked more like a swimming pool, actually. One by one I opened each bottle and watched the pills spill into the artificial blue toilet and settle at the bottom of the bowl. For a moment, the panic appeared—fear of the impending thing. I considered fishing them out and drying them off. But then I remembered how those small white pills had come to control every waking moment of my life—*for the rest of your life*. I remembered how they hadn't helped me keep my job or make up for the time I'd lost. I flushed and watched them swirl and disappear in the whirlpool.

Back in my bedroom, I stood in front of the full-length mirror trying to see if I looked different. I looked at this woman and thought of who she had been these last few months, wondered who was left. I couldn't go back now but still I wished it hadn't happened, or rather that it had, only differently. I had wanted this "help"—this diagnosis, these doctors, these pills—to get me somewhere, not take things away. I wished I hadn't had to break to this point; it was too much of a break, too loud, too public.

The pills were for the rest of someone else's life. Not mine.

This was going to be okay.

Right?

As Hopeless as Smoke

I'S NOT ALWAYS A storm. Sometimes it's a mist that descends from the sky, coating my body with faint wisps of despair. Or it's like walking out of my house and into a spiderweb that winds itself around my head, so that I spend the rest of the day swatting at my face and arms trying to brush off this phantom creeping. Or an uncomfortable itch in that space between bone and flesh that makes me want to remove my skin and hand it off to someone else, makes me want to peel my fingertips and expose blood. Anything to make this hushed suffering louder because when it's quiet it doesn't feel real.

This thing doesn't attack me with waves and quakes. It's a slight trembling. A disorientation. A confusion. *I must be confused.* Depression is a building falling on an ant. It is a hurricane in a thimble. It is not quiet. It is not vague. This is something else.

This is something else.

⚏

ANXIETY IS ITS OWN creature. Anxiety asks me to focus on the terrible things I've done. The people I've hurt. The promises I've broken.

Anxiety tells me to make a list. Mistakes. Regrets. Lies. A litany of shortcomings, a coil tightened, ready to spring.

Even when the best things occur, when the sun is angled just enough to offer light or there is beauty somewhere shining in the distance, the voice says—*This will not last. You do not deserve this peace. Remember that time . . . remember how he cried . . . remember how she shook with disappointment. Remember how you break everything you touch.*

✳

SOMETIMES IT'S A FOG. A quiet.

This is something else.

This is something else.

The Day Before

N Union Square, Manhattan the buildings curved into themselves like a Dalí mistake. I was walking in circles. Literally: down 14th, left at University—no, right—down to a left at 13th, left and then another left and back on 14th. I circled the block at least six times, walking a different way each time, hoping I wouldn't raise suspicion from anybody who happened to be glancing out their high-rise windows.

The circling was calming. Predictable. I counted my steps around each block and then multiplied that by how many times I'd gone around to calculate how many steps I'd taken total. I needed to keep my brain busy. I was concentrating so hard on my steps that I didn't hear my name being called until a hand grabbed my shoulder. My heart dropped, the familiar swirl and dip of an anxiety attack hitting me as I closed my eyes. I opened them slowly, hoping I was steady. It was Diane, a friend I'd known since she was a teenager in the New York poetry community. It was embarrassing to have anyone I knew see me like this—jeans falling off my hips, my jacket unzipped and hanging open. I suddenly noticed how the wind pushed its way into my body and shivered with cold. Diane looked at me with pity, her eyes registering quickly that something wasn't right. "You okay, Bass?" she asked, studying my face for more clues.

Had I been staring at her? I didn't trust my voice so I nodded.

"Where you headed?"

I shrugged, then took a breath that caught in my throat, so that my exhale sound like a choking. My eyes immediately filled and Diane wrapped her arms around me.

"What's wrong?" she asked, half hugging me, half holding me up. "What's wrong?"

My response was lost somewhere between my throat and the world, and she led me into the restaurant we were standing in front of. I sat beside her quietly with my eyes on the world outside the window. When the waitress came by, I stared at my hands folded in my lap, afraid to meet her eyes, afraid to offer another human being a glimpse of my broken.

"May help you?" she asked, her accent eliminating words and letters from her pronunciation.

Diane ordered the pad thai, then looked at me. "You want anything?"

I shook my head and whispered, "No." The silence that followed my answer shamed me into looking back down at my hands.

"When was the last time you ate?"

"Monday," I said.

"It's Thursday."

"I know." I didn't know.

The waitress excused herself, but returned seconds later with water before disappearing again. She moved so quietly and quickly, I had a hard time figuring out if she'd been there at all.

Diane wouldn't stop staring at me, so I wouldn't stop staring at my hands.

"You should eat."

I shook my head no again. "Not hungry."

Diane picked up her glass of water and pushed it towards me. "Then water."

I picked up the ice-filled tumbler, my hands trembling, spilling water all over the glass and bamboo table. "It's cold. I'm anemic," I said, hoping it would excuse the shivering. It was true, but even I didn't believe myself.

"Have you been taking your meds?" she asked me.

"Yes," I lied.

"Have you been seeing Dr. Tiago?"

"Yes." The truth this time.

Diane began to say something but stopped when the waitress returned. She placed a steaming plate of pad thai in front of Diane and put down another bowl in front of me.

"Lemongrass soup. You eat. On the house. Make you feel better."

I looked up to meet her face. She was older than her hands. Had the soft kindness of a grandmother or an auntie. She smiled sweetly, patted me on my back, and walked away. I felt as though I could hear my heart rattle around my ribs like a pebble in a cage. I stared at her retreating figure until she disappeared through the double doors.

"Bass?"

There was a thick, frost-like coating over everything. The world began to lean into me, the walls falling into themselves. I turned to look at Diane, then back to this bowl of soup I didn't ask for, then up at the walls falling into themselves and towards me . . .

"I have to go." I hear the chair topple over as I rose. The wood met the floor in a chaos.

Diane stood and grabbed my arms before I could leave. "Talk to me." Her words and her grip were firm. "You're scaring me. What's going on?"

I looked at my friend and I could barely manage a quiet "I don't know" in return. Before she could respond, I said, again, "I have to go," and rushed out of the restaurant onto University. I could hear Diane calling me.

I started to run down 14th Street toward the 2 train. I ran like everything was behind me. I ran like I was trying to leap out of my body. I ran until I hit the light at 14th and 7th and stood panting as car after car raced by, just blurs of color. The pounding in my ears. The city laughing and smiling without me. The cabs racing to make the light. The curb. The urge to step into the street again, walk to the middle and wait. I put a foot out and a man in a slick suit grabbed my hand. "Hey, watch out now! You don't wanna get hit."

No. I don't.

When the light changed I walked to 7th Ave. and descended into the train station.

#

THE CLOCK ON THE DVR read 11:00 P.M. I needed to sleep. It had been days, and even then, I hadn't slept longer than thirty minutes—broken into two fifteen-minute increments. I walked past the green couch that housed me for all those days and decided the bedroom would be better for tonight.

My room looked like a hurricane had hit it—the bed unmade, the sheets pulled away from the mattress, the floor littered with paper—poems I thought I needed to memorize, scraps torn from journals with lines scribbled in some foreign language—and an explosion of clothes carpeting the hardwood floors.

"I need to sleep," I told the postcard of Malcolm X on the wall, and next to him, Zora Neale Hurston agreed. I fell on the bed, not bothering to move any of the clothes or papers from underneath me, then kicked off my orange Pumas and got comfortable with the ceiling. The nightstand held the small lamp I'd paid too much for at Urban Outfitters, and when I opened the top drawer, I found the orange and white bottles, empty of the medication I needed. I picked one up and found the wastepaper basket across the room.

"If I make a shot, I'll try to sleep."

I sat up in my bed, recalling my old basketball days, and held the first bottle nestled in my right hand, left arm bent. The small pill bottle became a regulation-size basketball. I pumped twice, imagining I was on the free throw line of a championship game. The score was tied. Everything was resting on this shot. I lifted my arms above my head and tossed the bottle in a perfect arc. It almost hung in the air in slow motion, my hands still in release, floating across the room.

The pill bottle bounced against the wall before it hit the ground. I picked up another bottle and threw it across the room. Then another, launching it towards my mirror. I hurled the third into my open closet. Each throw felt like a stoning. When I ran out of empty pill bottles, I started throwing shoes and watched as they scuffed the white walls. I threw anything I could find until my arm was tired and my face was drenched. Every tear felt like another humiliation, another signal that there was something wrong with me. I rooted in my underwear drawer for my stash of Ambien pills I'd hidden from myself one lonely night when all I wanted to do was sleep. A night like tonight.

"I'm only going to take one," I told the James Baldwin postcard, his wide eyes peering at me, all pensive and disapproving.

I counted the pills in the bottle: eight. It usually took two pills to give me about an hour of sleep. I grabbed a nearby bottle of water and swallowed one. I took another, avoiding Baldwin's judgmental eyes, and cleared my bed as best I could. I took another, removing paper and clothes and—for some reason—a toothbrush from the mattress. I took another and changed into my plaid flannel pajama bottoms and a tank top, then lay down. I thought of the stars I couldn't see from Brooklyn and decided to practice a poem I needed to memorize: *trying to fall asleep confronted by the glow of a television at 2 A.M. or 3 A.M. or 4 A.M. is difficult/you cannot sleep comfortably here but your bedroom is just too lonely/too far way; too cold . . .*

╫

I woke up facedown on the wooden floor, my cheek pressed against the rug. I hoped I could stay down there forever. There was a loud pounding, a throbbing pain in my head, and a dry and heavy tongue. As the pounding continued, I realized it was coming from outside my head. I reached for my cell phone, but the screen was blank, the battery dead. The pounding continued, this time out of sync with the headache creeping around my skull, and I realized it was coming from the front door. I struggled off the floor. It felt like my brain and body were on delayed motion; everything heavy and slow. It took me years to make it to the door.

"Who is it?"

"It's Diane."

Diane. The night before began to present itself in careful order: circling the block in Union Square. The cold. The restaurant. The soup. Diane.

"I've been calling you all day."

"My phone died," I said as I opened the door. The words oozed out of my mouth like a stench. "Wait. What do you mean 'all day'?" Wasn't it morning?

"It's four in the afternoon, Bassey."

Did that mean I'd slept? Did it mean I was awake?

More flashes from the night before returned. 14th Street. Running. Baldwin's judgmental gaze.

One pill. Two pills. Three. Four. The phone before it died.

"I came to make sure you were still alive."

I wasn't sure.

"I'm fine," I said.

I let Diane in. I sat on the couch and Diane slid into the chair next to me. I tried to come up with something normal and sane to say as I stared at the wall in front of me. I searched for words and ways to tell her I was fine. The drugs were still making their way out of my system. I could barely keep my eyes open but my mind had started its sprint.

"I'm fine. I was just really tired, yesterday. And hungry. And stressed out, I guess. I haven't been working so money too, maybe? And people are mad at me, I think." I shook my head, trying to slow the words down so I could find the right ones. "But I'm okay. I don't need to see anyone."

Diane flinched but she stayed silent next to me. I shook my head to clear it so I could start again. I shook my head again so I could lose the crazy that was crawling up my spine. I shook it again and again and again, until I was on the floor with my head in my hands, shaking and shaking and shaking.

Diane got up and stepped into the kitchen. I could hear she was on her phone, but I couldn't remember how to quiet my brain enough to listen. And then the tears came. And then the panic hit my chest.

"Come on." She wrapped her arms around me and stood me up. "Let's go wash your face. We need to get you to Dr. Tiago's office. She's expecting us."

I don't know how we got from Brooklyn to the Upper East Side, where we met Dr. Tiago in her office. The rest was a blur of phone calls and activity. Dr. Goodman was called. I think Dr. Tiago handed me the phone because I remember someone telling me that we needed to get to NewYork–Presbyterian Hospital. I couldn't argue. I was empty and still leaking nothing onto the floor. Dr. Tiago walked us outside and hailed a cab. She may have pressed a twenty-dollar bill into one of our hands. Did I even have my wallet? Did I have anything?

I remember Dr. Tiago leaning into the cab and telling me, "It's going to be okay." She said to Diane, "Make sure you don't leave her. Make sure she gets checked in before you leave."

My head was quiet. I had stopped feeling. I was a body soaked in Novocain. Numb. I managed to look up at Dr. Tiago and then Diane and say, "Thank you," before slumping against the window of the cab.

We Don't Wear Blues

THE EMERGENCY ROOM: THE FIRST NIGHT

T SMELLS THE WAY I imagine death does. Stale. Thin. Like the air has forgotten how to move. This is the kind of place that will steal your spark, and that scares me more than the thing that brought me here. There must be something here that makes everyone who has passed through give up a part of themselves. It would be easy to succumb to white walls and obstinately shiny linoleum floors. This place smells like death and hopelessness and ammonia.

I have been here for four hours.

#

I WISH I COULD just stop crying. The security guard reads from a textbook and seems to hear neither my sobs nor my "Excuse me, sir?" When he finally thinks paying attention is worth it, he turns around.

I'm startled by his sudden interest but barrel through my questions.

I wish he would have remained with his back to me because everything I ask for is denied and dismissed with "Sorry. I ain't make the rules." I hope he fails his exam.

Diane is in the waiting room. I feel guilty for making her wait. I feel guilty that she had to bring me here. I always feel guilt when people are worried about me. I've been told that guilt is normal. It probably is; I just know that I'm not.

The waiting room is just on the other side of the door. I don't know what Diane is doing but every once in a while I can hear her voice echo from the hall.

"Can I just see her?" I hear Diane ask.

I'm hoping she'll get through, but the security guard rejects her requests as well.

⚜

I AM SO TIRED that the fatigue is fluorescent, casting a dingy shadow around me. I wonder what people will say.

I sit at the edge of a thin mattress waiting for someone, anyone to come in. I can hear a soft moaning from somewhere down the hall; I want to block it out, but I was instructed to leave the door open. Outside, there's a steady parade of nurses and doctors. None of them knows my name. They huddle outside the door and talk to each other like I don't exist. I'm not sure if I'm supposed to be hearing this.

"So why is that one here?"

"Severe depression and potential suicidality."

I'm digesting the word *suicidality,* adding it to the list of words in my head right before *adumbration* and right after *euthymic.* I'm playing with these words, saying them over and over. Allowing them to roll around on my tongue. I do this whenever I hear a new and interesting word. It's the only normal thing I've done since I got here. My game is interrupted when I hear "Room One" and "twenty-eight years old" and "underweight."

A few of them glance in my direction and I fold my arms across my chest. They all remain huddled around the door.

I shouldn't be here.

✳

TWO HOURS LATER SOMEONE finally actually enters the room. It's the attending nurse. She tells me she has only come to take my vitals. I don't know what that means and am not sure if I want them taken. I have nothing but these paper scrubs. When they are wet, they stick to your skin like shame. I pull the top up before the nurse sees the way my collarbones struggle up through my skin. The tag reads "XXL" so it quickly falls off my shoulder again. At least now there's no more crying. I don't really feel anything anymore; just a slight swimming in my head.

I don't realize that the woman has taken my temperature and blood pressure until she's already done. The nurse asks if she can take my blood.

"Only if you buy it dinner first," I say, under my breath. It's my first joke in days. I want to keep what little spark I have left. The nurse ignores my stab at humor; I fall silent again. I can tell she is new by the way she turns and taps the inside of my elbow, searching for a "good vein." I don't know what the difference is. She finds one that must look like it will behave and slides the needle in. No blood comes. She removes the needle again and attempts to find another vein and another and another. They are all empty.

I wonder if I'm already dead.

I close my eyes, hoping my lids will act as dams against the tears. The nurse ignores all of this—she is still searching and stabbing. I am only trying to keep breathing. She, finally, finds an open vein and the blood seems to pour out of my body like it's been waiting for its freedom. She gives me a self-satisfied smile. I watch the red race through the tube and fill the vial. I'm not sure I'll have anything left.

I start to ask her a question, but she's done with me; instructs me to hold a square of gauze and then tapes it to my elbow. This will stop the bleeding. I close my eyes and wipe my face with the back of my hand. So much for not crying. I swallow and ask, "What should I do now?" but she's gone by the time I look up. I press the gauze and tape hard. Something about the pain makes me feel alive.

I'm alone again.

And still, no one has asked me my name.

⋕

TIME PASSES. ANOTHER NURSE enters.

"Ms. Ikpi?"

I stare at her blankly, hearing her but unable to recognize the name as my own at first.

"Bassey," I finally say. "Ikpi, yes."

She says, "Ordinarily, I would give you a psych evaluation but based on Dr. Goodman's recommendation and your . . ." Her voice trails off. "We're just waiting for a room to open up."

"Based on what?" I ask.

"Just sit tight. We'll get someone in to see you soon."

"Based on what?"

The room begins to spin, and I can feel the beads of sweat forming on my forehead. The heat starts to radiate from my chest and spreads. I want to take off these scrubs and this skin and pick at my flesh, but I know the answer to "based on what?" is that I'm crazy and that this is what crazy people do. They take off their clothes, they pick at their skin, they look for ways to run. I lie on the bare cot and curl into myself. The panic and the tears meet, and I have no energy to talk myself down.

"Your friend left." It's the apathetic security guard. I don't look at him. "She wants me to tell you that she called some people for you and she'll be back tomorrow."

I don't move. I hear him turn to leave and offer him a low "Thank you. Good luck on your exams."

DAY ONE: NIGHT/EARLY MORNING

I'T'S MAYBE THREE IN the morning. I've finally been admitted. I have nothing but the shameful blue scrubs and my fear. I'm in a wheelchair. No one will tell me when I get to leave. The nurse who wheeled me up said, "You haven't even been here yet. How would we know when you get to go?" I couldn't answer that, I just twisted the hospital bracelet around my wrist. I've been reduced to a condition.

I don't want to be here. I've never been a patient in a hospital. I've only been to the hospital to welcome newborn babies and to see my mother at work. She's a nurse that smiles.

I'm wheeled onto another floor and parked at the front desk. As the nurse who brought me in disappears into the hallway and the heavy ward door closes with a click behind her, yet another nurse appears in front of me. She shows me the plastic bag that holds my wallet and cell phone. She says things, but her words are muffled and distorted. When she asks my name, I look up and study her face. She has her pen poised to write it down, but when my mouth opens, a sob escapes and I retreat into a space behind my brain again.

#

I'M ALONE. THE BED is small and lumpy. I'm grateful for my own room, but the quiet is unbearable. There is no television. There is only the sound of my heart pumping much too fast. The panic has begun to pace itself at least. I feel trapped and try to figure out how to breathe. Inhale then exhale then inhale then exhale but my heart is beating too fast and my brain confuses the rhythm of breathing so that I'm choking, trying to inhale and exhale at the same time. There isn't enough room in me for tears. My fear is humid and thick.

I lie flat on my back under a thin, scratchy blanket. It is so cold here, but I refuse to change into the regulation white, cloth scrubs. I don't want to feel like I belong here. I close my eyes and try not to think of the number of bodies that have been in this bed, the number of people who have pulled this same blanket around them. I can't think of these things or I will never rest. Sleep is as impossible as privacy here.

#

I'VE BEEN HERE FOR two hours. The door to my room is a constant metronome of opening and closing. I've already learned how to time it. Can figure out who and why before they step into the room. The ones checking beds fiddle with the knob before they enter. There is one Jedi sweep of their flashlights and then they are gone again. The nurses arrive more quietly and quickly. They are in the room and by your side before you notice that you are no longer alone. They're a bit better. They take your temperature and blood pressure and some ask how I am and look like they would listen. Others ask and turn their heads away immediately. I've decided not to say anything to any of them. I don't want them to know. Besides, I know that it's all in the charts they carry.

⚏

I'VE BEEN HERE FOR four hours. Everyone who enters the room reminds me that it is a weekend. "Our usual doctors are out. You'll soon meet the weekend team." All they're saying is that no one can help me yet. So, I just nod. I am afraid to speak. I am waiting for my family to arrive. I am waiting for my friends. I am waiting for someone who will speak for me. My voice has betrayed me too often.

I need someone who will care. These people do not; they can't. To them, I'm just another patient. Just another faceless body on a conveyor belt of afflictions.

DAY ONE: MORNING

THIS SILENCE IS ANYTHING but peaceful. It sounds like the walls hold muffled screams. Like there is something waiting just beneath the surface. I watched morning arrive through the window across the room. I stayed awake waiting for the explosion. I can hear the other patients outside of my door. They can't seem to hear the truth about this quiet. It's not soothing or peaceful. It creaks and groans and smells like the end of you. I refuse to sleep here.

DAY ONE: AFTERNOON

HAVEN'T MOVED FROM MY bed. Nurses have come and asked me to eat or join the others in group therapy, but I shake my head. I want only to lie here until I'm told I can leave or die, whichever comes first. The nurses deliver messages from my doctors; they say, "Bassey, you have to try." In my head, I answer, *at least I'm not dead.* I'm not sure if this is better.

I daydream. Stare off into space and think of places I'd rather be. Sometimes, I hold conversations with myself. It helps me organize the rapid tumble of words in my head. Provides an internal monologue that keeps me present, not careening into the dark and disappearing. I'm asking and answering questions to myself, in my head. In the middle of a sigh and a nod of agreement, a doctor enters. I am shy once again. I can't tell if he's seen this exchange. I hope he doesn't think that that is the problem.

He studies my chart and asks me if I have a history of heart problems in my family. I nod and say, "Yes, but only the broken kind."

He doesn't look up but throws a low, tired chuckle in my direction. I imagine that he is sixteen hours on an eighteen-hour shift; that he has been yelled at and threatened in the last hour alone. *At least this one makes jokes*, he will think. He will tell the others how I'm different. He will tell them that I have a spark. He will say that there is nothing wrong and let me go. I'm so lost in my fantasy that I am startled when he turns to face me.

"Tell me what brought you in today."

I want to say "a cab"; something else to encourage a laugh or a smile. He looks up, waiting for an answer. I don't know what to say. I've been here for hours and no one has asked me anything that isn't clinical, that is when they've asked me anything at all.

I swallow, hold my breath, and exhale. "I don't feel good." My voice betrays me and I start to cry. It had been forty-five minutes since I last cried. I was going for a record: one full hour. I don't want them to see this. I don't want them to know that this is what happens. The doctor sits patiently waiting for the sobs to shorten. I'm sure he has been here before. He shifts his weight. I want to believe that he is resisting the urge to hold and comfort. This only gives permission for the sobs to attack more violently. I am shaking and weeping and tired and ashamed and scared and alone. I'm angry with myself—I cracked for this one, the others think I'll crack for them too. He pats my knee and offers me a Kleenex. It's all that he can do. His job calls for distance. I'll only be a medical chart after he reaches for the door. I take the Kleenex; refuse to get attached.

He asks me again, what brings me here. I swallow and shrug my shoulders. "I don't know."

DAY ONE: EVENING

MY FAMILY AND FRIENDS have come and gone. I thought that I needed to see them to feel better, but their presence only made the fear and loneliness even bigger. The fear on their faces terrified me. Their forced platitudes and words of encouragement frightened me even more. Diane comes with magazines. Maysan comes with food and concern. Syreeta comes with pens and a pad. My roommate, Maro, comes with my Sidekick and questions. My father wanted to know what had happened so he could fix it. My mother wanted to speak to everyone on staff. I wanted to tell them that it was all a big mistake, that they'd release me as soon as they realized. My sister didn't understand, and it is she who I want to understand more than anyone else, to understand me. I want her to not feel shame. I don't want to be the fucked up, crazy, older sister. I want her to be proud of me. I want her to understand why I'm here, that this isn't all of me. I want her to be able to explain it to my parents but my voice is locked away somewhere. I don't like to worry people. I didn't want to trouble them with concern so I smiled as often as I could, laughed when it was called for. I avoided questions that I couldn't answer. Deflected questions to answers that I didn't want them to know.

"I'm going home on Tuesday. No matter what," I told them.

My mother begged me to stay until they could help me, until they could figure out what to do. So I would never have to come back here. I nodded. I didn't tell them how frightened I am. I didn't tell them how long it's been.

I nodded, said, "Yes, Mommy," until she was satisfied. It was worth it when I leaned into her and put my head on her shoulder. We are not a physically affectionate family, so her small hand wrapped around mine felt like an embrace. I wanted to tell her that the nurses don't smile but I wasn't sure she'd understand. She is a nurse that smiles, if not always at me.

They stayed until visiting hours were over. I needed them longer than that. They told me they'd be back. I wasn't sure if I believed them. This place makes it difficult to trust anything. I didn't tell them that. The nurses told them that I don't eat. They told them that I don't talk. My father wanted to know why. My mother demanded that I do.

"They won't let you leave unless you follow the rules," she said.

⧉

THE WEEKEND DOCTOR HAS authorized Ambien for me. An orderly brings it to me wheeled on a tray. He asks my name and then hands me a plastic medicine cup with the familiar pink pill in it. I stare at it. My heart squeezes and pulsates, remembering the last time I took these pills, the night before Diane came for me. He offers me a small bottle of water, but I refuse and swallow the pill dry, tossing it back like a shot of tequila. I close my eyes and open my mouth wide as he inspects my gums, cheeks, and tongue. When he's satisfied, he turns and leaves. I can hear the trolley squeak and stop next door.

I lie back and pull the blanket up to my chin and stare at the lines in the ceiling. I pretend I'm in Brooklyn, in my bed, in August. The moaning outside my door morphs into the steel pan band practicing for J'ouvert. I tell myself, this year I will go to the Labor Day parade. This year, I won't complain about the noise. I push away the swell of anxiety as I remember the hordes of people in colorful costumes pushing their way down Eastern Parkway. I will pretend I don't mind crowds. I will actually live and not hide once I get out of here. I just need to get out of here. The colors blur into nothing as my thoughts swirl into a drain. I close my eyes and give in.

DAY TWO: MORNING

OOD IS STILL DIFFICULT. I only manage a dry roll for breakfast and the plastic-tin-covered hospital juice. Still no regular doctors. *It's the weekend, you know?* I mouth the words with everyone that says them. I hope they don't notice. It will be another reason to keep me here. I make a mental note: next time, I will only go crazy during business hours.

Today, there are huge spaces between crying. Today I ask a question: Can I have a one-on-one instead of group? The nurse my mother asked to look after me is shocked but doesn't have the answer. She tells me that she will "ask the weekend doctor." We finish the sentence together. I tell her not to bother. She doesn't want to let go of the fact that I'm speaking. She asks me if I want to come into the lounge or get something to eat. Maybe I'd like to meet some of the other patients. I shake my head. I'm fine.

"You're going to get bored. You can't stay cooped up in your room forever," she says.

I remind her that I can. "It's one of the reasons I'm here."

She nods and exits the room quietly. I didn't mean to be rude, but I don't belong here. I'm not like the others here, still I'll do what they ask but just so that they'll let me leave.

Activities are mandatory and the announcements for them serve as time markers: community meeting at 10:00, lunch at noon, group therapy at 1:00, yoga at 2:00. If I close my eyes, it could be summer camp. The woman screaming that she's Bill Clinton's wife reminds me that it's not.

Adhere to the phone rules. Be patient with the nurses. Be on time to group. Put your linens in the hall hamper. Put food trays on the cart. Put your left foot in. Take your left foot out.

DAY TWO: AFTERNOON

THE WEEKEND DOCTOR TELLS me that group is mandatory.

"You don't have to participate if you're not ready, but you need to be there," he says.

The nurse could have told me this.

DAY TWO: EVENING

D EVICES THAT TAKE PICTURES and record sound aren't allowed. My cell phone does both, so they took it when I checked in. Thanks to Maro I have my smuggled Sidekick and charger. She knew that I needed it. It is my only link to the things that make sense to me. I'm careful with it. When the nurses come, I hide it under my blanket or pillow. I'm not sure if the Sidekick itself is allowed, but it's all I have, and I won't risk them taking it away. I keep it stuffed into the toe of one of my boots. Sometimes, I put a dirty sock on top so that even if it's picked up or inspected, you still can't see what's inside. The sock is filthy. The nurses cut their eyes at me and wrinkle their noses. I don't care if they think I'm dirty. At least I have the only thing that I need. This is the only rule I will break. I want out of here too much. Coming here was a mistake. I don't belong here.

DAY THREE: MORNING

T HE WEEKEND STRETCHED ON for months but it's finally Monday. The fabled "regular doctors" are making their rounds. I can hear them across the hall, laughing with one of the patients. I noticed him earlier. He's always parked at a table, hosting guests like he's at a dinner party not in a fucking psych ward.

For the first time, the fog is beginning to drift from me and I'm suddenly aware of where I really am.

Mental hospital.

Crazy house.

Loony bin.

I can feel shame begin to crawl down my neck and grip my shoulders. It's suddenly too bright in here and the air is too small to be shared with all the people in the room, the unit, the hospital . . . the world.

This was a mistake.

"Excuse me!" I call out to the first person in scrubs that walks by. I gather myself as she stops, trying to fix my face into something sane and capable. I imagine what Oprah might look like if she was in this situation and I offer a small, endearing smile. She returns the smile and it gives me hope that I'm doing this right.

"Yes?" she asks.

"I'm sorry. There's been some kind of mistake. I have to leave."

She smiles again, this time her face is open with such pity that I want to punch her.

"I don't belong here." I try again.

"Why don't you head down to the lounge? I think there's a movie starting."

"I don't want to watch a movie. I want to go home." The words are coated with a panic I'm doing my best to contain.

She smiles again and walks away. I need to get out of here.

※

WHEN ANOTHER NURSE SUGGESTS that I join the others in the rec-reation room, I agree. I need to get out of here. She blinks back her shock and moves quickly, afraid I might change my mind. The laughter floating into my room makes me second-guess myself, but I follow her across the ward.

The recreation room is roughly the same size as my room. There is a shelf full of board games and puzzles. The bookcase is anemic and barren.

"They don't allow any books that might make us crazier. It doesn't leave many options." I turn and see the man in the wheelchair who was laughing with the doctors earlier. He's at a table not far from me. I can't place his accent, but I know it's not American. I stare blankly at him, not sure if he's speaking to me. My eyes drift from his face and I try not to flinch when I notice he only has one leg. I open my mouth to say something but close it again.

"Name's Trevor," he offers.

"Bassey."

He smiles. "Pretty name that. So what brings you here?"

I look away. I don't want to be rude but I don't know what conversations are supposed to feel like in here. I lower my head and leave Trevor in the room.

"Bye, Bassey," he calls after me.

I pretend I don't hear him.

DAY THREE: AFTERNOON

THE REGULAR DOCTORS DON'T care either. They talk to each other, not to me. I'm angry at them for taking so long to get here and then for forgetting that I'm not a case study, that

I'm more than the medical charts they cling to like needy children clinging to their parents. I am tired now. My sleep is still slow to come and often interrupted. I have little use for these well-rested, well-groomed doctors and their questions. They've already been told about me, have spoken to my doctors in the outside world. They still offer treatments that I know damage my body. I know my body, I tell them. I know what makes me feel worse. I will not take anything they give me. They insist. I tell them that I'm sensitive to medication. They nod and make notes.

The youngest looking one begins his sentence, "We were thinking of putting you on Geodon . . ." I've told him already that I can't take that, it makes me numb and groggy. And the other one brings headaches. And that one makes me tremble so much that I can't sit or sleep. And the other one upsets my stomach so much that what little food I allow entry erupts out of my mouth like punishment. They stare at the bones poking from my shoulder blades. They scribble furiously into their pads. I tell them that I want to talk to my doctors. The woman with the thin, pinched face and the bleached blond hair of an 80s popstar reminds me that my doctors are not here. I tell her that neither was she the last few days. I want to be seen by people I trust. You lot can continue taking my temperature and blood pressure.

The one with the Payless shoes and homemade haircut does most of the writing. He is too young to look so haggard and weatherworn. He sighs and tells me that this treatment has worked for countless others like me. I tell him that I am not countless others and he doesn't know what I'm like. I want my doctors. I want someone who understands my body and my reactions. I want someone who will listen to me.

I want to leave.

They write furiously in the books. I know they are labeling me as difficult. I don't care. I hate them all. All the anger I feel is betrayed by the tears streaming down my face. I am terrified and shaking. Why won't anyone notice this? They all stand and watch me weep. Like I'm not real. Like I'm performance art at MOMA. I hate them even more.

One of them says, "We'll leave you alone now and try to get your doctors on the phone." I manage a thank-you as they file out of the room. The door snaps behind them. Aside from the bed checks, I am left alone for the rest of the night. I'm not sure if this is a punishment or a reward. I try to be grateful for this pocket of quiet, but it creates a loneliness that recalls the curl and crying of the first day. It reminds me of what brought me here.

I'm starting to no longer feel like myself. I don't want to be here.

I need to work harder at being normal.

DAY FOUR: MORNING

'M RELIEVED WHEN I'M woken up and asked to go to the pharmacy. Dr. Goodman has called and prescribed Wellbutrin and Lamictal. Meds are dispensed every morning at 7:00. I stand in line with other patients as we shuffle up to the pharmacy window. I don't see Trevor.

It's the first time I notice that there are only women on this side of the ward. Some of them rock from side to side muttering to themselves. The woman with the black turban stares blankly into space. There's a woman so skeletal that she's skin stretched around bone. I wonder how she exists without flesh. I try not to stare, but I can't seem to understand how she's still alive. I look at my own wrists and remember how much I want to starve myself into nothingness. My plan has been to disappear and here she is, half my size and still here. I'm disappointed on her behalf.

The guilt fills my face and I do my best to keep my eyes down and my arms folded. I wonder if they look at me with pity. If they say, "Look at her. Did she even try?"

When it's my turn, I swallow the pills one by one and open my mouth for inspection. I want to go back to my room and slide under the covers. But I have to try.

The dining area is around the corner from the pharmacy. I'm a vegetarian so my food isn't with the others'. My dietary restrictions are how I got away with eating in my room the last few days. Vegetarian food just means they leave the meat out of the same meal as everyone else. My friends visit every day and bring me lunch and dinner, so it's only breakfast I've had to endure.

I've been sliding in either too early or just as meals are ending to avoid the others. But now it's eight o'clock, rush hour here. The chatter from the room is enough to get me to turn back, but I have to try.

I have to try.

Breakfast is two slices of dry toast and pats of butter and congealed grape jelly and an elementary school carton of milk. I bite into the toast and chew slowly, surveying the room. Most of the others are quiet, but in the corner is the skinny woman from earlier and two other people; one of them is laughing loudly. Trevor. He catches my eye and shoots me a smile. I'm immediately pissed off. What the fuck is he doing here? We're all fucking crazy and sad and weird and he has one leg. Why is he so fucking happy?

I look away, grab the toast and the plastic cup of juice, and leave.

DAY FOUR: AFTERNOON

'M IN THE LOUNGE. The nurses and doctors come by occasionally to tell me how pleased they are to see me out of the room. I've finally remembered how easy it is to pretend to be normal, so now I perform for them. I tell them what they want to hear. I admit that I need to be here and say I'll give treatment my all. I'm telling the truth, but I'm lying. I search my brain for the right words to say and the most *she-doesn't-belong-here* way to say it.

Maysan had brought me takeout from Zen Palate and a stack of gossip magazines. She also brought a pen and a journal, but I don't have any words yet. I'm in the lounge so they can see me eat. I read the magazines and pretend that I'm in a café in the village and not in a psych ward on the Upper West Side. This would be easy, but the lounge is filled with sick people and their visiting families. There is a woman whose husband visits her for hours every day. I've seen her wandering the halls. She is pale and quiet, dressed like the Hasidim I see in Crown Heights, pushing strollers filled with groceries and babies. Her husband visits her for hours. He comes in the morning and stays until the nurses encourage him to leave, reminding him that he can return the next day. He talks to her, holding his black hat in his hands, his hair covered with a small black yarmulke, his blond ringlets brushing his cheeks as he speaks. I pretend that they are in this café with me. The three of us are not here. She never responds, only stares past him. Sometimes she gets up in the middle of a sentence and walks away. He always rushes to catch up with her. They stroll the hallways together like they're in a park.

DAY FOUR: EVENING

t's ELECTION NIGHT. A group of us gather around the small TV in the recreation room. I'm still the quiet one, but I'm there. The plaid couch holds me and Anorexic Amy. Once again she's twirling her brittle hair around her fingers. I see Trevor playing Scrabble with one of the attendants across the room, uninterested in America and our politics.

George W. Bush is declared the winner. I wish that I could cry, but I know we're being watched and I don't know how upset crazy people are allowed to be about things like politics. The others disperse to their rooms for bed checks, but Amy and I have been declared "well" enough to be afforded a few special freedoms. One of which is being allowed to watch TV beyond curfew. I sit frowning at the TV as the news anchors drone on.

"But we're the crazy ones," I mutter to myself.

Amy makes a soft strangling sound that concerns me. I turn to look at her and I see her tiny shoulders shivering slightly. It takes me a moment to realize that she's laughing and still twirling that hair around her fingers. She stares at me, her wide gray eyes falling into her face while skimming mine.

"What do you do?" she asks suddenly.

I open my mouth to respond, not sure what to say. I no longer feel like anything I supposedly am. Who was I four days ago? Before I can speak, she adds, "I'm a lawyer. They say if I gain ten pounds, they'll let me go home." Then she gets up and walks out of the room, leaving me alone with her question.

Trevor wheels up and parks next to the armrest. I get up to leave before he can start a conversation. But I can't make it up in time; I'm still thinking of Amy's question.

"Why are you here?" I demand.

He recoils at the force of my question. I repeat myself, hoping to take the bullets from my words, but they fire again. "Why are you here?"

"What are any of us doing here, love?" he responds, his voice thick with Ireland. We are staring at each other in some sort of showdown. I sit down in the spot Amy just left, far from him but still there. The quiet sits between us waiting.

"I wanted to die but my body wouldn't let me," someone answers. It takes me a moment to recognize my own voice. I say it again, "I wanted to die but my body wouldn't let me."

Nurses, doctors, friends, and family have all asked me the same question and I've given them one false reason or another. But this is finally the truth. I wanted to die that night and many nights before then.

I stare at the wall just to the right of the television. "I'm just so tired, you know. Everyone is so disappointed in me." I force a coating over my body and step behind my mind to direct the tears elsewhere.

"Do you wanna know how I lost my leg?"

I nod.

"I'd been having a shite time of it at home. Everything was just turned to shite, but I wanted a grand adventure. I wanted to see New York before I went so I bought a one-way ticket. Then a few weeks ago, I was on the platform, bleeding drunk, waiting for the six train, and I saw the light in the tunnel coming towards me and I jumped."

"What? You jumped?"

"Yup"—he laughs—"I jumped. Ended up under the train."

"Did it hurt?" I ask, knowing the question is stupid even as I say it.

"No. Well, probably, actually. I don't know. I think it hurt so much that my body shut down. I think I was certain I had died but then I woke up in the hospital. Fucking alive, mate. Except for my leg. That was still under the train." He laughs again. That laugh. How can he laugh about this? I don't know how to react, I can't even summon up a nervous giggle. I just stare at him. Laughing at wanting to die. Laughing about jumping in front of a train. Laughing about his missing leg. He laughs so loudly and long that I begin to question my inability to laugh with him. "Imagine—you have an entire plan to fucking die and not only do you fail, you end up more fucked than when you started."

I can feel the sting of tears appearing. The sound of his laughter creeps up my leg and wraps itself around my stomach. All I can think of is his bloody, chuckling leg left behind on the 6 train track. Before the sick feeling can make its way up my throat and all over the plaid couch, I get up and walk away.

His words follow me into my room, through the closed door, under the blanket, into sleep—*imagine ending up more fucked than when you started.*

DAY FIVE: MORNING

W HEN CAN I LEAVE?"

The doctors are back. They've asked me all the same questions they asked yesterday and the day before that, the same questions the weekend doctors asked me on Saturday and Sunday. The same questions with the same answers that were in the charts with my name emblazoned on the back.

"When can I leave?" I ask again.

"We have to make sure that the medication is working and you're no longer a danger to yourself."

"I never was." Their pens scribble furiously on paper. I shift my weight and correct myself. "I never was a danger to myself. I was just tired and sad. I just wanted to sleep and stop crying. I've done that. The meds are working. I'm eating. I'm sleeping. I'm talking. I learned how to play Scrabble. I still hate Scrabble. I'm okay. When can I leave?"

"We'll get back to you after we study your chart and progress."

I pinch my thigh discreetly to prevent my frustration from being an outburst. I summon my Oprah smile and respond, "Of course! I just wanted to let you know that I was feeling better."

They all nod in unison and shuffle out of the room. I wait until I hear them next door, before I fall back onto the bed. I want to scream but I know that I can't. I can't cry anymore. They have to let me out.

DAY FIVE: AFTERNOON

ONE OF THE DOCTORS has returned. He asks me if I'm willing to be interviewed by some psych students. I didn't know that the hospital was connected to Columbia University. That explains the horde of note-taking doctors. If I'm well enough to talk to people, does that mean I'm well enough to leave?

"We can discuss that," the doctor responded.

DAY FIVE: EVENING

THE RECREATION ROOM IS empty. I finally want to write. I don't have anything to say.

DAY SIX: MORNING

THE NURSE CALLS ME to the front desk and tells me to get dressed.

"Am I leaving?"

"No. You're going to speak to some students."

Right.

I hope I showered. I don't remember. I was allowed my own clothes a couple of days ago. No more shameful scrubs falling off my body. I sleep in my jeans. It's cold here at night, and the blankets are so thin. I put on the suede boots from Edinburgh, the ones with my Sidekick and charger stuffed in the toe. I hesitate, eying the nurse watching me dress.

"Can I have some privacy?"

She nods and steps outside, leaving the door slightly cracked. I slip the contraband into my pillowcase and fold the blanket on top of it.

We go through the back. Down a corridor connecting the hospital to the school. We end up in a classroom. Students. A professor. Me at a table in front of them. The girl in the green sweater asks me a question. The boy in the purple T-shirt asks me a question. The professor has on a sports jacket. He asks the students a question. Somebody's hand shoots in the air. He calls on them.

People are talking about me.

I'm there but I'm not.

Questions.

It's an audience. I perform. I answer their questions like I'm being interviewed. Like there's a camera and a live studio audience. I'm charming. I'm funny. I'm smart. I'm sane. I'm just like them. Better. I'm better than them. Green Sweater speaks again. "Do you think that you'll ever be able to live a normal life?"

What?

DAY SEVEN: MORNING

'M LEAVING TODAY. THE doctor pulls me out of the dining room during breakfast. I do my best not to be too happy. I don't want them to change their minds. I'm doing well. The meds. No reason to keep me any longer. Insurance. No longer a risk. Follow-up appointment with your doctors. Can someone come and get you? No. It's too sudden. I'm okay. I can get home. Okay. Go pack. Paperwork.

DAY SEVEN: AFTERNOON

THE NURSE LEADS ME through the lounge. The other patients look up; I avoid their eyes, feeling guilty that I will soon be on the other side of the electronic door, just a week after I arrived. Some of them have been here for months. I've managed barely a week. I tell myself that it's because I'm doing well. The meds are working—I can feel my brain slowly connecting and gluing itself back together. But I can't stay here another day or it will all start to shred again.

I thank them and sign the paperwork that says I'll continue to take my meds and see my doctors. They tell me I'm leaving on my own recognizance. I've always liked that word. I begin to play with the way it feels in my mouth but catch myself. The admin is staring at me, waiting. I can't give him a reason to keep me here. I will myself to be normal but my hand jerks as I try to write my name and age and date and time. "Meds," I quip.

He doesn't return my laugh, hands me a plastic bag. Slips of paper with prescriptions scrawled on them. My cell phone. My copy of *Lady Sings the Blues*. My wallet. He asks me to count the money inside to verify it's all there. I don't remember how much is supposed to be in it. But I check the box that says it's all there anyway. No holdups.

The door buzzes and I hesitate before stepping through. It slams and clicks behind me.

I take the elevator to the ground floor and into the lobby of the hospital. There are too many people around and I can feel my heart squeeze with panic. I zip up my cardigan, put my head down, and head for the exit. Has the sun always been this bright? This persistent? This present? I flag down a yellow cab.

Brooklyn.

Some Days Are Fine

SOME DAYS ARE FINE. I wake up determined to move through the hours like someone born with all their bones intact. Other days, I wake before the sun and lie in my bed staring at the ceiling, patiently waiting for the tears that have greeted me every day for weeks. Minutes pass and nothing comes to wet my face.

I know this place.

After months of slow descent, an excruciating decline to destruction, the fog has lifted. I am in that small slivered space of "better."

※

SOME DAYS ARE FINE.

I move through the world like someone born with all their muscles intact. Depression is no longer a thing that squeezes my heart. It does not threaten my life. It does not drown me. It does not try its best to eat me. This is when my brain knows the truth and reminds me of it.

This is when I'm finally able to hear the advice that people, kind but uninformed, offer. This is when you tell me to take a long walk to clear my head, suggest I eat something to get my energy up, tell me to think happy thoughts, and I can do it. This is when you ask how I am and I can say, *better*.

This is better.

❋

PEOPLE LIKE TO USE the metaphor of darkness when it comes to depression. My experience is more like a fog. A thing descending slowly. A thick *something* that surrounds me, distorting my vision of myself and the world around me.

❋

PEOPLE CONSTANTLY ASK HOW I'm doing (now). The *now* is silent. They try to make it sound like they're just saying hello, making small talk, being polite, but the worry always dots their foreheads like perspiration, the concern coats their skin with a sheen, the beads of sweat that appear when you've climbed one stair too many or when the summer heat is just a mild nuisance and not the drenched and wet affair of a heat wave. The worry is a slight rise in temperature. I can hear them wrestle with the questions, can see how their faces struggle to make their concern something more casual. I can hear the fear in the intake of breath before the questions. Like the split second of silence before an explosion.

❋

MY FAMILY SPENT YEARS looking at me and not knowing that I was not okay. When they saw how bad the "not okay" could get, they rushed to treat me like glass. Not something broken—like I felt—but something they had never noticed was in danger of breaking.

I'm home from the hospital. We are in the kitchen: My father kneels between the island and the microwave, nervously opening and closing the cabinet below the counter, waiting for an opportunity to speak to me. I am filling my water bottle at the cooler in the corner. I watch as he pulls out a mixing bowl, then replaces it and then pulls out a colander and replaces it. When my bottle is dangerously close to overflowing, I know I cannot avoid him or his questions anymore. I stand and focus all my attention on the bottle top. I am concentrating on this twisting and tightening like it will defuse a bomb or like it will keep the question from finding me. "How are you doing . . . ?"

My dad stands before I can figure out how to avoid him. I lament not bringing my phone along as a diversion tactic. He repeats, "How are you doing . . . ?" *(Now.)* His eyes quickly scan my drawn face, my sharp, pointed collarbones, the way my sweatpants hang despondent and fearful around my hips. He inhales and draws in his bottom lip and forces his eyes back to my face. He won't ask if I've eaten. That's my mother's job. He waits for me to answer.

"I'm doing better." I attempt a smile then change my mind and stare at the bottle I am twisting in my hand. The cold and wet feels like an acceptable sensation. I am trying to isolate the cold and the wet—feel one and then the other.

"Ups and downs," I say to our feet.

My father's feet point towards me and then away, his casual is filled with too much purpose to make me comfortable.

"The downs are still up enough to keep me moving . . ." I hope this sounds like a reassurance. I hope this stops the incessant opening and closing of cupboard doors. I hope this quiets the *now.* "These feelings don't disappear overnight."

My father grunts some encouragement. I use the pause after to flash a smile of "I'm good. I'm fine. Don't worry" before I make my escape from the kitchen.

#

THESE FEELINGS DON'T DISAPPEAR overnight. They can quiet. They can ripple. But they don't disappear.

There are two sides to this—the fog and the hurricane. The fog has been my worry and concern because it is the thing that attempts to erase not just me, but my memory of it as soon as I'm feeling "better." It's like nothing happened, right? It's like it never existed. Almost.

It must have passed Better in the hallway on its way out. Maybe they greeted each other with a head nod.

Better: Can I clock in now? I've been in the lobby waiting.

The Fog: You came up a few times.

Better: To check on her. Make sure you didn't overstay. I brought some temporary smiles and reluctant laughter, remember? But then I left again.

The Fog: Cool. I'll lay low for a little bit. You got this. Don't get too comfortable though. I'll be back.

#

SOME DAYS ARE FINE.

Those days I need to monitor how much electricity is running through me. I need to make sure that my brain isn't on a high-speed chase with words, that I'm not leaping from idea to idea, danc-ing within myself. I need to make sure that my bank account isn't drained at 3:00 A.M. because I needed to have every MAC lipstick mentioned in the dozens of YouTube tutorials I just spent hours ob-sessing over. I need to make sure that there is no paranoia, no fear that everyone might be angry with me so I need to send as many text messages as I can to clear up this invisible slight I may have caused. I need to make sure that the fog hasn't been lifted only to welcome the hurricane.

That is a different kind of destruction.

⋕

SOME DAYS ARE FINE.

Depression is easy. It comes as hard as thunder and destroys. Ma-nia is the seductive one; the one you're not supposed to fall in love with.

Then there is a switch. The space where they all meet: anxiety, hy-pomania, depression. It becomes more difficult to fall asleep, yet my eyes fly open an hour, sometimes two, before my alarm and I just lie there, staring at the blurred walls or ceiling of my bedroom. I am forgotten. My heart leaves my body. I am unimportant. My noth-ingness floods my chest, the list of my missteps over the last few decades pushes into my head and whispers, *You are a failure.*

I can spend hours and weeks on all the mantras: *You are loved. You deserve to be here. You are needed. Necessary.* I can chant these affir-mations a million times in constant and consistent repeat until one day the record skips and *no you're not* becomes the new song and I become limbless, I evaporate into nothing.

I've lived with depression my entire life, sliding in and out of it as easily as I do the size 2 pants that only fit when the fog has made its way back. Depression is like a rumor that grows quietly and steadily, causing no problems or distractions until, one day, I remember that time I left the stove on and the burnt food and the smoke and the chaos of the alarm that blares a broken jazz in my mind because this shame is the only soundtrack I have.

♯

I TAKE MY MEDICATION faithfully. I do all I can to make sure that this thing does not eat my bones. I visit my doctor twice weekly. I am trying to stay alive.

One day, I wake and instead of dread, instead of the echoing, hollow sadness, instead of a stomach that lurches in disappointment at morning or at waking or at the twenty-four hours I need to occupy, I feel a calm, I feel a soothing. The sun appearing and allowing in the beauty that I have made it into morning. This happens every single time, until it stops and the fog comes again, like clockwork I wish I could smash into bits. And this, right there, is the one thing that I can count on—no matter how long it goes away for, it will always come looking for me again. It will always return.

♯

I AM SO TIRED of this returning. I tell people words that fall hollow on my own ears. A friend told me once that each of us and our unique fingerprints hold up the universe, that any missing fingerprint is a loss the universe can neither regain nor afford to lose. I share this with people often. I give them the suggestion *Allow yourself morning*. I tell them it means that today may have been a rolling ball of anxiety and trembling, a face wet and slick with tears, but if you can get to morning, if you can allow yourself a new day to encourage a change, then you can get through it. *Allow yourself morning.*

I do my best to remember this, but the older I get, the more I wonder what the point is. When I was in my twenties and early thirties, I accepted that this thing would return. I treated it like a benign tumor that insisted on growing back. I still had my whole life ahead of me. I'm forty now, and I am tired of fighting this thing every single time it appears. And it keeps appearing, despite the twice weekly appointments and the twice daily rounds of medication. It keeps appearing.

#

I'm tired. I'm tired. Those of you that I love know
who you are. May God bless you.

—Phyllis Hyman

#

YOU ALWAYS WAKE UP optimistic. Your eyes fly open, you lie in bed and you think, *I feel okay. Maybe I'm okay.* You get up and take your meds. You sit on the bed and collect yourself before you leave the room. You wonder why it's so dark. Is it the weather? There was a storm all night. You reach over and turn on your phone—you turn it off at night to allow yourself silence. You wait for it to boot up. It says 4:40 A.M. You slept for three hours. You try to go back to sleep but you're awake now. You're just awake. You grab your laptop to do some work. You don't have any. You finished yesterday. You're waiting for feedback. You lie back on the pillow, stare at the ceiling, and let the tears roll back into your ears. "It's not always like this. You're usually just fine. Just wait," you say to no one. We will believe it again soon.

This thing wants to eat you. Don't let it. It's exhausting. Rest if you need to. It is a liar. Believe only that you are necessary and an important part of this world.

⧻

I KNOW WHAT COMES with quiet.

I've learned to love so quietly that some people forget that I ever loved them at all.

I can be "too much."

It is this "too much" that forces the quiet.

This bipolar. This many-sided creature. This life of mine. This brain I was gifted. This brain that drains. This brain that protects me even as it scolds. This brain that is mine, in all its broken and fractured and bruised and bullied. This brain constantly in conference with the racing heart, reminding me to slow down, stay calm. We will not welcome the hurricane.

⧻

I'VE BEEN THINKING SERIOUSLY about a goodbye. Perhaps even slowly preparing myself and my family and friends for it. It's not on any daily "to do" list. It's not listed below "buy toothpaste" or "finish book chapter." It's not today or tomorrow. It's nothing I'm looking forward to. It's just an appointment, like my biannual dental cleaning.

I've lost a few people to suicide—I know, all too well, how these losses leave holes in the hearts of loved ones but I also know that after a few weeks, the tears slow and after a few months, they stop. I know that after a year, birthdays and holidays still bring grief but also that in order for the brain to survive, eventually, the grief leaves. Eventually, those who grieve me will live without me. They must. It isn't fair but it is honest. But I try and I push past the desire to leave and just remain, broken and bloody. As Auntie Phyllis says, "I am still looking for one good reason to stay."

Because I know how that dog-eared page persists and insists you return to it. I know how the brain and the heart and the spirit fight daily to stay in the book and not write themselves out of the story. I know. I know. I know.

This is a rambling something for the friends that have passed on, the strangers that followed them, the loved ones I celebrate earnestly in private, the birthday that looms, the love that subsists on violent silences, the truth of this getting older . . . and being older. And feeling older and watching everything and everyone around age as well. It all feels like a long winter. And as a child of summer and sun—born with too much fire—winter is not a season that can go on too long.

When We Bleed

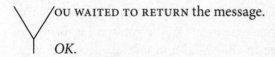OU WAITED TO RETURN the message.

OK.

You probably said more than that. I hope you said more. I'm sure you gave details and condolences and let your grief spill and splinter and become poetry and movement. You didn't just say *OK*. Because it wasn't even *Okay* but *OK*.

When Peter died, your spirit flipped inside out. Your brain, always your protector, said, "We can't survive this. If you feel this, if this enters you, we won't be able to survive it and before all else we are about survival." This is how your body cares for you. How we rally for you.

Peter is dead.

You know the message said more than that. You know that there were details and condolences and a spitting and sputtering mess of grief.

Peter is dead.

Not *Peter died.*

Or

Peter passed away.

You remember it as *Peter is dead* so that's the way we remember it.

That was the gist. That was the point. That was all.

#

YOU WERE IN THE bedroom they said was yours in the new house. They'd moved while you were away. While you were in Brooklyn carving out your space in the world and letting the world carve something out of you. But you left Brooklyn. You were overwhelmed by rent and medical bills and the choreography of staying sane. And now this benign growth in your uterus.

Remember how you found out? How the sudden itching and discomfort in your panties led you to your first nonmental medical checkup in years? Though it had been a year or two, or a week, or two days since the last time someone filled and discarded and filled you and there were condoms, always condoms, still, you worried about the possibility of disease and disgrace. You worried and welcomed the possibility of a new shame that would replace the ones you already carried. So when you went to check about the itching and the doctor asked about laundry and allergies and you remembered that the laundry service had changed detergent, you were relieved. You were disappointed.

Before you left, she asked you about the growth. You stared dumbly at your breasts and then your belly wondering where there could possibly be a "growth" prominent enough to be asked about. She asked you to lie back and pressed her hand against your belly. "Here," she said. She guided your hand and covered it with her own. "Here," she said again. And you felt the hard something. "How could you have missed it?" she asked you, even as you asked yourself. She told you that you needed to schedule a scan or an MRI or whatever it is that people use to check these things. And you made the appointment knowing that you would never go. Who had the time or the money? But you were obsessed with that growth. You named it Chuckie. You spoke to your mother for the first time in four months because she is a nurse who should know what to do about these things. She was surprised to hear from you. You could hear the joy beginning to grow in her voice but you stopped her. *They said it was a growth.* Something poking or growing or morphing or ready to explode. She told you to come home and you had vowed four months ago to never return but that was before there was a grapefruit growing. She told you that there would be another doctor and the scan or MRI or whatever. "I'll pay for it," she said. So you went home and you acted like nothing had happened. Like you hadn't vowed never to return, never to visit, and now there you were. Preparing to remove an organ you'd never really wanted.

You refused to unpack your belongings. "I'm not staying long," you said.

⌗

PETER IS DEAD.

You are in the bedroom that's now yours in your parents' new house. The grapefruit is now a cantaloupe. All the doctors ask, "How can someone this small not notice something this big?" All of them. You tell them that you don't know. You told one, "I've recently started eating." He blinked at you and then blinked away, unsure.

Peter is dead.

We don't want you to forget. You are on the brink of something pulling you into the center of yourself. Where it's safe. Where there are no fruit-shaped things in your body. Where Peter is alive and on your couch in Flatbush or standing in the mirror in the hallway, his hair a constant art project, gold framing his face.

Peter is dead.

You cannot let this enter you. You know that you won't survive it. We know. So we allow you a rocket and not a submarine. We offer you an explosion instead of a submersion. You have space, here, to lie on the floor and wail into the empty, undecorated bedroom they say belongs to you.

Peter is dead.

Will we let her cry?

Yes, but not too much. No spilling over. No leaking or drowning or wading.

We need to take her to Brooklyn.

But she can't stay. Not where there will be crying and wailing and reminders.

Peter is dead.

She will want to leave. Find a reason to leave the world.

Don't let her. Hold her above it and live in the middle: somewhere between okay and not okay.

But let her feel it. Let her feel something.

⋕

YOU GO OFF YOUR meds. Again. But this time you don't plummet, you stand. You stay.

Peter is dead.

You want to feel every broken bottle and jagged rusted blade of it. You don't want to mask it. Don't want to ignore that your body let you live.

Peter is dead.

I need to know what it feels like to lose like this. To have a reason to fold and fail and fall.

⋕

YOU CANCEL THE OPERATION that would remove the grapefruit-turned-cantaloupe. Or whatever fruit wants to invade the body next. You buy a ticket to New York for the next day or the next week. You just know that time has passed and then the funeral is the day the New York transit system shuts down for a workers' strike.

All of you gather in a church.

Peter, our Santeria priest, our Elegba trickster, is supposed to be in the room with us. He's not. It is the first thing you notice when you walk in.

You see the polish and gleam of the wooden, satin-lined coffin. You trace the curve of the wood, spend a moment admiring the smooth. You are too far to see the body. Too far to make out the face above the suit that belongs to the body in the box.

Peter would never wear a suit.

You have never seen him in one. You will not let the last time you see him be the first time.

If you had stayed a moment more, you would have melted. You find your friends all standing, huddling together as far from the front of the room as they can get.

This ceremony is not for Peter. He would have asked for a celebration. A Lauryn Hill song echoing around the rectory. This isn't for Peter. There's not enough magic or music or laughter. This isn't for us. There's not enough Peter. So you turn to face the coffin. You see the face. You see Peter.

But you don't.

You decide it's not Peter. You need to believe that when Peter left, he turned into one of the stars you count. He disappeared in a cloud of spark and fireworks and shot across the sky.

You don't know who or what was in that suit not being a sparkle and magic but it wasn't Peter. It isn't Peter—I don't care what the collective hearts in the room sound like breaking at the same time.

✳

WHEN PETER DIED, I was in my bedroom at my parents' house. I was sitting on the floor, staring at the ceiling, wondering what it would feel like to have my belly sliced open and an organ removed. Would I feel hollow? Would my liver and kidneys and pancreas wander around in search of the missing?

⋕

I'M DRUNK. MY FRIEND is having a party in her penthouse in Union Square. I knew after the second drink that there would be four or five more. I needed to ensure that I would feel nothing.

There is a guy at this party—his face familiar but unremarkable, hair was soft like Jason's. His skin the same freckled and pale. My mouth doesn't know or care about the difference. He has me pressed against a wall in an office or a bedroom or against a refrigerator in the kitchen. Then in an elevator and then the lobby of this posh building. In the cab, I straddle him immediately, grinding my pelvis against him. He has been hard since he saw me and won't stop kissing me like it's a surprise each time.

"I can't believe we're doing this," he whispers into my hair.

"Shut up," I exhale into his mouth.

I know the cabdriver is watching us. I know he thinks I am ill mannered, badly-raised, maybe slutty. This is what I want. I have spent my entire life trying to be seen as a "good girl," trying not to shame my family or destroy my image, but being a good girl didn't stop me from going crazy and it didn't keep Peter from being dead. So fuck them. Fuck everything. Fuck everyone.

Fuck me.

He lives in Brooklyn. We fall into his apartment. He wants to pull me into the bedroom but there's no time. On the floor. He scrambles around for his wallet, his hands trembling slightly. I grab it from his hands. Rip it open and hand it back to him.

Fuck me.

I slide against his body and guide him inside me.

It's not enough.

I pull him into my mouth, my tongue encouraging another awakening. I stop before there is nothing left and say, "Condom," into his ear. He returns with a box. I want to laugh but there's no time. Again. Then again. He tells me he can't do it again. He tries again to find my mouth, but I turn away. He's of no use to me now. He slides down my belly to wind a tongue around my right nipple then the left. His ceiling is a mottled off-white. It is raised and bumpy like pale, diseased flesh. The texture begins to make me feel ill, so I look away. The movement encourages him. His mouth is just below my rib cage and then my navel. I can feel his breath move the hair between my thighs, feel his tongue begin to root and dart as he teases his lips on me. No. I don't want his mouth on me. I want him inside of me. I want him heavy against my belly and ribs, I want his weight. I wiggle my hips away from his exploring mouth and twist and roll until his head is rested on my belly. I move again and he pulls himself up, a plank hovering above mine. He is still not where I want him.

I'm trying to picture his face now. Trying to collect his features and tell you that he had a freckled nose or plump lips or small wrinkles on his forehead. I want to tell you that his hands were strong and his fingers long and elegant. I want to tell you about his hair, whether it swooped across his face or was close against his scalp. I can't. Because I don't remember. He is nothing but weight and grief and wait and grief.

"You don't want me to eat you out?" He says it like I just turned down a winning lottery ticket. I try to keep my eyes from rolling and my mouth from shooting off a slick, sarcastic response. I shake my head.

"Let's just go again."

"I can't. I really can't. Let's just sleep. Maybe in the morning." He rolls into me and puts his arm around me. When I can hear him sleep, I slip out of his arms and find my clothes in the dark of the room, picking up condom wrappers and sticking them in my pocket.

There will be no morning.

I'm in some part of Brooklyn still negotiating with last night's alcohol. I walk to the corner against the wind waiting for a black car or a yellow cab finding its way back to Manhattan. It's cold and I never have gloves, so I stick my hands in my coat pockets and finger the condom wrappers. I'm not sure why I picked them up. Souvenirs. Trophies. Proof of my willingness to self-destruct. Of my willingness to drag my blood around the city.

In case you forget.

In case you ever fucking forget.

I signal every passing car hoping one of them will be a jitney driver. Two cars pass me. The cold has shocked me into temporary sobriety. A black Cadillac slows, the man rolls his window down and asks, "Where ya headed?"

I don't know. Where am I going? I give him Syreeta's address. I pray she's home and awake.

He nods and I slide into the backseat. The heat catches me off guard after the face-blistering cold I just left. My phone begins to ring and I look down. I don't recognize the number and I don't pick up. There's a message—"Hey, where'd you go? Are you coming back? Uh . . . call me back or . . . I mean . . . Yeah. Bye." The phone begins to ring again with the same number. I stop the call and block the number. It's too hot in the car for it to be so cold everywhere else in the world.

And Peter is still dead.

"Can you pull over for a second, sir?"

He barely maneuvers his car to the side before I open the door and vomit.

Searching for Magic

S O THIS SADNESS RETURNS quietly. Always quietly. No great trumpeting or horn blast. No drum circle or full-bodied gospel wail. No stunning metaphor or dazzling simile. There is only this throbbing and distant and empty and quiet. Always this white noise of rush and tide. It's what silence sounds like. Water.

I've been trying to figure out some way to create poetry out of this heavy, hollow something. But times like this, when it feels like even the words don't want me, I am hard-pressed to understand my purpose. Beyond the baby boy, who gets me laughing and smiling and sometimes exhausted and wishing for time machines through it all. Even when I put him in the high chair and turn on *The Backyardigans* or *Wonder Pets* for ten minutes to disappear into the hallway and press cheek against knees to stop the tears before they appear.

There has been blessed little crying. There was a moment last week, after the car broke down in Baltimore. There was a distinct and persistent wetness on my face, a thick in my mouth. And I allowed it. Hoped that this flooding over would be the end of it. That the water would overflow into that empty space and fill it with something. Anything but this loud and frenetic nothing.

I pretended that I was crying for a him. Pretending that it was a cracked and bruised leftover heart that was leaking motor oil all over my hoodie. I needed an easier reason to cry, why not a him?

There is no him. Just me.

I've been hiding. Pretending this thing no longer exists. Pretending I can carve a little bit of "normal" out of this. Shape it into something more palatable, more acceptable. More readily understood. Replace one word for another and pray no one notices how purple and bruised my hands are from clenching my fists. How quickly the words tumble uncensored. How often the debit card is emptied. How there is a new obsession every other day. This need to face a blinking cursor and call it writing. Or a Facebook page and call it writing. Or Twitter and call it writing. Or text thread and call it socializing. But it's really about this need to own something daily. To have a place I need to be, where I will be missed if the status remains the same for three hours.

And there is the baby boy who misses me when twenty minutes go without a song. Without a new dance. He is attaching himself more these days because he knows this sadness is here. Remembers it from before, so he will not sleep unless the mama is lying beside him. Will not eat unless the mama holds a fork as well. So I am trying. I am lifting myself out of bed every morning to assure him Cheerios and Pinky Dinky Doo and Hip Hop Harry and the only nursery rhymes I know sound suspiciously like Tribe and Black Star and Jeff Buckley and De La Soul and Lauryn Hill and Sam Cooke and when he hears the first three lines of "Billie Jean," the baby spins and laughs because he knows already. And one day, I hope he will forgive me this. Because I know he knows when the mama puts him in the high chair for ten minutes she is probably in a hall somewhere pressing her cheek against her knees.

This thing ain't easy. And I don't mean to complain because this life is beautiful and it's magic. And I am blessed and grateful. But this brain feels broken sometimes. This brain does this thing that takes little soap bubbles of "everyone feels this sometimes" and morphs them into latex balloons of "you're the only one in this world who can't seem to lift herself out of bed in the morning" and then the balloon becomes brick and the brick becomes wall and the wall is a mountain and then you're stuck. So I'm grateful to only be latex balloon right now.

But this thing ain't easy.

Four years ago, January was the first time. Chicago. It got me. I was in my dressing room, before the show even began and I was flooding. I remember pacing and jumping and dancing and singing and trying to shake myself out of the tears but everything I did seemed only to make them come faster and harder until I was underneath the sink, knees to chest.

So it could be worse. It can always be worse. Silver lining.

It's not worse. It is this.

When the book remains finished but paralyzed. And the gigs are coming but not fast enough. And there is no money. And the baby needs clothes and shoes and private school and soccer cleats and a parent who doesn't welcome tears this easily, and I can't offer him any of that right now. And the emails and tweets and comments call me brave and inspirational, I feel like a fraud. Like, who am I to inspire or advise anyone? And I know it's not all true. I know it is the broken brain and the way it misfires that makes it feel true. I can feel you all rushing to comment with pep talk and reassurance and I love you for it. But I have to figure out a way to pop my own balloons. Or learn how to keep them as soap bubbles.

This desire to be "normal." To wake up one day and have a corporate career and a 401(k) and a savings account and a house on a hill and some kind of chicken recipe and a husband who mows lawns and tickles babies and comforts the woman who still feels like a girl, who needs something stable. Even when stable feels closer to death than sleep.

When it's not about men. But it is. And it's not about this writing that feels pointless. But it isn't. This life that is so beautiful and amazing and magic. But it isn't. This wondering why the alone keeps return-ing. Why the quiet is so loud today. Understanding that this isn't real. But it is. Knowing that I created it. But I didn't. This how did any of this happen? This back and forth trying to figure out how I came to this here. This mommy and daddy's house. This somebody's mother. This suddenly too old to live a life this untethered.

This far from Brooklyn.

Acknowledgments

K ANKE, THE OLDER YOUNGER sister, the strength and backbone. The focus and determination I could never conjure. Thank you is not a strong enough phrase for the gratitude I have for you. I watch you take space in this world and negotiate how you choose to enter it and I envy your courage. I know being my sister hasn't been easy. I have not been the example I've wanted to be but I've looked up to you and marveled at how gracefully and beautifully you move through this world. You have sacrificed so much for the family and I hope you know how grateful we all are. I will spend the rest of my life making sure you know how much I appreciate you.

Jesam, the wisdom and the logic. I remember I used to call you the Golden Child/the Genius. I see so much of Elaiwe in you. You hold both an empathy and a kindness in your eyes. Your generosity has saved my life. Your vulnerability has warmed me. Your support has encouraged me. I don't know the ways to thank you for your mere existence but I hope this is a start.

Kebe, the baby. You are the soul of this family. You are the spirit and the spark. I have always admired your bravery, your ability to carve space in this world for yourself and defy all objections. Your voice is the strongest and the clearest. You are brave and bold and when I look at Elaiwe, I see you. Your eyes, your wisdom, your strength, your ability to find the center of something and work and fight until you meet it.

Elaiwe, my actual baby. You brave boy. You are the best of all of us. Thank you for choosing us to be your family. You are hugs and love and you have given me the strength to accept both. "We are not a family that hugs" but you are a child who offers and leans in and gives us all a reason to find warmth in each other. I love you for who you are. You are perfection and I hope you know that, whenever there is a doubt, you are loved more than you can imagine. I am so proud of you, Boogie. I want you to always know that everything you are is a gift to this world. Never forget that you are a magical somebody. I can't wait for you to grow into the power you possess and change the world with your love and your kindness and your empathy and your brown boy wonderful. You are love in human form.

To Mommy and Daddy: Thank you for not giving up on me. I hope I still have time to make you proud. Thank you for loving and accepting me, flaws and all. Thank you for recognizing and giving me the literal space to re-center and regroup and try and try and try again. Thank you for being the kind of parents who may not approve but always will, ultimately. Thank you for teaching me how to "love anyway."

I love you all so much. More than I can adequately put into words. I would not exist without you. All I want is to make you proud, to ease the burden that I've placed on you time and time again. This is just the beginning for us. We got this.

To Akwaeke, my editor and friend: This book, literally, would not exist without you. Thank you for being the first person to see my scrawling and random thoughts and stream of consciousness, and for saying,

"You have a book." You are a treasure and a wonder of a being. You put so much heart and soul into this project when I was still in severe doubt and denial about what it was or what it could be. Thank you for your friendship, for your belief in me and in this project. I cannot begin to repay you for all that you have given me. Thank you for offering me sanctuary and The Sanctuary. You are beauty and grace and kindness, and I cannot wait until the world sees all of you. They ain't ready.

To Erin, my editor: Thank you for believing in this project and wanting to see it published. Thank you for pushing me and giving me permission to tell this story in a real way. When we first spoke, you asked me, "Are you ready to go there?" and I said, "Yes," but I didn't know what that meant until we got started. Thank you for always wanting what was best for me and this project, no matter what form that took. Thank you for fighting for me and for seeing me and yourself in these words. Thank you for fighting for YOU and choosing to get up and live, every single day. We did it, Wicks, and we're still here.

Thank you to the team at PS Literary, especially, my agent, Eric: Thank you for taking a chance on me. Writing a proposal had me paralyzed for years and you had it done in weeks. I know the book I wrote isn't the book you sold, but you stepped in when I had all about given up hope: on writing, on life, on everything. You were part of what started my journey back to myself. I will be forever grateful. Thank you to Steve Clark for taking a Facebook joke seriously and sliding into my DMs with "You need a book agent," and then leading me to you. Thank you, Steve.

Matthew McNerney: The best part of this book might be the cover. I don't know how you took my "I don't know what I want" and turned it into the best thing I could imagine. You are brilliant, but I think you know that. Thank you for being such a supportive friend and shoulder to cry on and for bailing me out in more ways that I can mention here.

You've given me so much (including Bruno Mars tickets) and I hope that I tell you that as often as I can. I'm running out of space here.

To Tosin Aje-Adegbite: You have been part of this journey since the eighth grade. Thank you for never bailing on this trip, even when I wasn't the best friend I could be. You were one of the few who understood my heart before I could understand it myself. You have forgiven me more times than I deserve, and I hope that you know how much I love you. We did it, sis! I'll be telling our full story in the next book.

To Nana-Ama Danquah: When I read *Willow Weep for Me*, I felt seen and understood for the first time. You are the blueprint for all of us black girls who struggled to put language to the chaos that we carry within us. You have inspired and encouraged and provoked and pushed and warmed me. We have been laughter and tears and the desire to keep moving despite it all. I am so proud to call you sister, mentor, friend, confidant, coach, family, namesake. Here's to more words, more love, more friendship, more truths. This is for Mildred.

Al Letson: My brother, brother, brother: Remember when we joked that we were permanent plus-ones at award shows? We were joking but we were dead-ass serious. It took a minute but we're both on the way. Dust off your tux. From the slam world to taking over the world, you have been my partner in crime every step of the way.

SQUAD: Thank you for offering me space. Thank you for welcoming me back. Duchess Lynne: Thank you for being the big sister of my heart. You taught me to always choose myself and be unapologetic in my quest to exist on my own terms. Because of you, I learned to trust my voice.

Syreeta from the Clan McFadden: I never told you this, but it was your encouragement almost two decades ago that inspired me to keep writing. You were one of the first people I showed my non-poetry writing because your opinion meant so much to me. You read "Hasaan" (now "This Is What Happens") and I still remember how your feedback made me feel. You have so much to give us and I'm ready for the world to see it.

Sir Roger: Where do I even start? You saved my life. You gave me Chicago, three years ago, when all I wanted was an unending nothingness. That invitation invited hope when I thought all was lost. You are my family.

Patrick: Thank you for your calm and gentle spirit. For your wisdom and your wonder and that pure, pure, pure heart of yours.

Patrik-Ian Polk: Three years ago, our lives were so different. We spent so much time trying to figure out how to get from point A to B. I've watched you take your rightful place as a legend in the industry. Thank you for being my friend and my family and for telling me to keep going and showing me what it looks like to persevere and never give up hope.

Dike Uzoukwu: You already know. I'm so proud of you. I know that by the time this book hits the shelves we will have celebrated too many of your wins to count. You are more than just a friend to me, you are my heart. I'm so glad you choose to see sun. I'm just marking this spot so you can't fake like you don't know me when you blow up. Also, delete our iMessage chats, please. It's for the best. I love you.

Tarana Burke: I feel like I'm calling everyone family but if you're not family then I don't know who is. We have both come such a long way and I am so proud to see the world finally recognize who you've always been to those of us who love you. Thank you for always putting me in spaces that show me not only who I am, but who I can be. I'm so proud of you and I love you and Brown-girl Kai so much. Always here.

Alba Anthony: You are a truth-teller. You are all fire and brass to mask your golden soft center. Thank you for showing me both in equal measure. You have offered me the exact sequence of words to inspire and infuriate me at any given moment. Don't ever doubt how important you are to the people who love you. You are one of the best people this world has.

Yesha Callahan: We have been through a lot over the years. It's been such a pleasure to see you make and meet and match every dream you've had. Thank you for always extending the kindness you try to hide from the world. You are one of the sweetest people I know. You are thoughtful and generous and now I've told the whole world so you can't deny it. This is going to be a great year. Trust me, I'm exactly one day older, thus wiser, than you.

Thank you to the team at Harper Perennial: Megan Looney, Caitlin Hurst, Tracy Locke, Hannah Bishop, Stacey Fischkelta, Dori Carlson, Libby Hanks, Jen Overstreet, Mary Sasso, Amy Baker, and Doug Jones.

Derek Musgrove (you got a whole essay so this is all you get here), Courtney Hobson, and the faculty and staff at UMBC-Dresher Center for the Humanities for the summer residency for letting me spread my work all over the floor and giving me an office to work well into the night. Also, thank you for the snacks.

To those who are no longer here:

Erica Kennedy: Thank you for your strength and your courage. Thank you for telling me to "Just write, Bassey." Thank you for giving me permission to write the stories you didn't have the opportunity to write yourself. I miss you so much, Erica. I owe you so much. I'm so sorry the world is missing out on you. They don't have any idea how much they're missing. Thank you for bringing me Mimi and Aliah and Carolyn and Issa and Deesha and Denene and Helena and Nicole and the whole BB Crew.

Siwe: Baby girl. Look what we did! You inspired me to keep living and to keep going. I miss you.

Peter: My God, Peter. It still hurts and it will always hurt. I carry you with me always. WE did this.

My therapist Jennifer Chen for keeping me alive over the last four years.

The friends who have provided space and encouragement and love and light and support and laughter and truth over the years: Lara Asimolowo, Michael Arceneaux, Camille Robbins, Rod Morrow, Ijeoma Ogwuegbu, Mychal Denzel Smith, C. Jay Conrad, Christopher Macdonald-Dennis, Obia and Omini Ewah and the whole Ewah family, Sabrina Hayeem-Ladani, Imani Akram, Maysan Haydar, Melani Douglass, Anya, Avery, Krista, Huny, Cali "Calliope" Greene, Chinisha Scott, Issa Mas, Helena Andrews, Scotty, Diane Wah, Alice Smith, Evelyn Bandoh, Kola, Eghosa, David, Topher, Nadine at Easton's Nook, Margaret Whitener and Kennedi, Marie-Elizabeth, Ebony, Shannon, Remi, Bree, Titilope Sonuga, Tim Young, Ozoz, Pamela, Kecy, Kat, and Li'l SoSo.

Thank you to all the teachers, professors, musicians, artists, thinkers, healers, writers, readers, dancers, playwrights, actors, storytellers, therapists, doctors, and artists who have real estate in this. Thank you to everyone who has ever given me a word of encouragement or support. Thank you to everyone who has ever had to tell a difficult story. Thank you for telling those stories.

Out of everything I wrote, the acknowledgments probably terrified me the most. I did not get here on my own, I did not do this work on my own. There are the obvious ones, the ones who I can look at and know they directly impacted this work. The ones whose stories are told, the ones who allowed me to tell their stories, the ones who created these stories with me. There are the ones who saved me, the ones who held me, the ones who gave me space to break and mend and break again. The ones I hurt. The ones who will not forgive me. The ones I dare not ask forgiveness from. The quiet ones. The ones who hold themselves in my memory and nowhere else. The ones who fall through the cracks and slip away. There are so many and so many and so many because nothing I am or have been would be possible without tremendous support and encouragement from friends and strangers alike. I can't begin to name you all but I can't bear to leave you out. So, this is the compromise, and I hope it reaches you. These acknowledgments are for this particular book and these specific stories. Inshallah, there will be other books and other acknowledgments and other speeches and other opportunities to tell the stories of all the people in the universe who have brought me here. I hope there will be opportunities to tell you to your face but, for now, allow the gratitude to find its way from my heart to yours.

And thank you for reading this book.

Do me a favor: kiss both shoulders and the inside of both wrists.

Love someone and mean it,

Bassey

About the Author

Bassey Ikpi is a Nigerian American writer, ex-poet, constant mental health advocate, underachieving overachiever, and memoir procrastinator. She lives in Maryland with her soccer superstar son. www.basseyikpi.com.